Goddess Nest

Ananda Cait
Copyright © 2020 Ananda Cait Carver

All rights reserved.

ISBN: 9798676941536

DEDICATION

This book is dedicated to the Goddess who ventures deep into the wild jungle of her own dark shadow time and time again.

CONTENTS

	Foreword	iii
1	Elevation Poetry	1
2	Elevation Mantra	42
2.1	Inner-Child Healing	62
3	Elevation Ritual	81
4	Elevation Oracle Card	126
5	Goddess Love Note	174

"Beautiful is a Wombyn in Alignment with her Divine Assignment."

FOREWORD BY CLARITY BARTON

Ananda Cait is an angel with a heart of gold —- a true Goddess embodied.

I met her five years ago during my beginnings of running women's circles in Toronto based on archetypal initiation journeys of the divine feminine. She attended these circles religiously with a wide-open mind and heart and with much wisdom to offer our circle. I could tell that she was nourishing her soul with these archetypal stories; as if she was drinking them up to water her inner-garden.

I saw her integrate these teachings readily into her life and she became the conscious hero of her own journey, letting spirit initiate her and guide her deeper along her spiritual path. She followed this inner-guidance with much grace, courage and devotion.

What strikes me about Ananda is her ability to be herself and yet fully be guided by spirit in everything she does. She is a radiant being who always somehow shines. I've witnessed her commit to herself over and over again: always re-entering and connecting to spirit. She is a true healer & teacher who walks *The Path*.

My favourite memory of Ananda Cait happened one night during our Aruba Divine Feminine Retreat in 2019. That night, I witnessed her transform into her most divine-self as she blasted our circle with healing Reiki energy and bowed to the Moon, the Ocean, the Earth and to all of us as her Sisters — a true Goddess at work. It seemed to me that her life had become fuelled by spirit alone and that she was surrendering as a humble servant, letting divine energy flow freely through her whole being — I will never forget it.

I learned a lot by working with Ananda Cait and witnessing her. She is an inspiration to me and I am honoured to call her my Sacred Sister. I know that what she offers to the world comes from her own spiritual devotion, connection as well as her own sacred heart and life-experience. It is beautiful to know that I can always trust her to come from a place of integrity and divine inspiration.

May her words bring you closer to your own sacred truth, may the medicine that she holds transport you all the way back home to yourself, and may you too water the inner-garden of your soul with the divine feminine magic and wisdom.

Clarity Barton
Divine Feminine Empowerment Leader
Tantric Teacher & Spiritual Coach
www.AwakenedPriestess.com

GODDESS INTRODUCTION: PRAYER POETRY

Welcome Goddess to our magical & powerful book of ritual & self-reflection. If you have picked this book up—make no mistake—it is time to dive deeper & call in your higher-self: The Goddess within.

As we move through the first chapter of Prayer Poetry I ask that you stay curious about the concept of softness. What does softness mean to you? This could mean many things, but the true awakening happens when we are willing to let go of that which we cannot control and fall deep into a nest to be cradled in deep reverence, embraced for all of our phases and ultimately healed within.

The first chapter, 'Goddess Prayer Poetry' is a channeled expression of free-writing that was transcended through my channel of light after sinking deep into a conscious meditation. I feel these writings have been passed through me to you by the Goddess archetype herself. For 20 years I have been channelling these writings and saving them for my own ritualistic healings. I began to set up pampered spaces where I could meditate and adorn myself with the many abundant gifts Mother Earth provides us with.

I began to call these spaces *Goddess Nests* and if one of my soul sisters was having a heavy day, I would help them to set up a Goddess Nest to cry, heal, laugh or to surrender in. These nests would always include different gems or talismans each time; whatever I was guided to most that day. I would allow a different Goddess essence within to guide me to the healing items I needed at that time: different flowers, crystals, fruits, sage, incense, books, blankets, plants and the list goes on.

More importantly, these nests have always been spaces of artistic creation that have held some of my darkest hours and some of my most celebrated moments of gratitude. These nests provide a physical home for our heart chakra to rise up and speak to us. These sacred spaces are also a place where we can have revelations, birth creations and be one with other sisters moving along a similar journey into the heart.

If you've ever needed a place to just be and meet the Goddess within, creating a *Goddess Nest* is a powerful way to communicate to the Universe that you are willing and ready to receive this connection and guidance from your higher-self. Think of the *Goddess Nest* you create as a bridge-point between the Heavens and Earth. It is a the physical manifestation of how you wish to feel and how you identify with yourself through the lens of love.

Like each woman, these poems reflect the many essences we hold within our energetic nature. A woman can be of any age, depending on the self-work she has practiced and integrated. A Goddess can also be any age and is dependent upon her faith and trust within ones-self, as well as the work she has done to embrace and release the pain she has carried throughout her experiences. All of this self-work is practiced in order to embody her higher-self and share this essence with the rest of the world. Ultimately the Goddess within us shows up when we are ready to become our highest version and share that person with the people around us. She is a teacher of sorts, but also a compassionate student that listens and is aware to the many signs of the Cosmos.

The Goddess is admired for her charisma and beauty as well as the way she serves and loves herself. She is also a woman who walks in her truth without apologizing, who knows her boundaries and exercises these boundaries with love and compassion. She knows that kindness is not weakness, but it is the core-route to showing up fully in life in order to elevate consciously. She embraces her anger proactively and takes time to process and create a healthy relationship with all of her emotions. It is this work that replenishes her energetic cup so she can easily flow with the river of life and not react-to or dive into the chaos that is inevitably available to us at anytime. In this way, she amplifies her auric-field and begins to attract what she is: Divine Love.

It is here where the Goddess can begin to understand that life is not about staying in the energy of love all the time, this is quite impossible, in fact. We know that as spirits experiencing a human life we will always shift into anger and resentment, but the lesson the Goddess ignites in us is how quickly we can come back to the power of Love by accepting the totality of our existence.

It is in these spaces where we can process emotions and allow the Goddess to awaken and guide us back home. This is why *The Goddess Nest* is so powerful. It is the time we create to process, embrace and proactively witness ourselves without judgement or fear.

Here, we can let go of the rest of the world, take off our masks and truly accept, forgive and heal from our past or present. We also have the opportunity to experience ancestral-healing within our wombs and learn about the ingenious story of our DNA lines. It's in this loving space we create for ourselves where we can accept, forgive, embrace and release any thought or emotion that will no longer serve us when moving forward towards our awakening and integration of the Goddess.

It is each and every one of our birthrights (yes, you!) to embrace the Goddess energy within and fall madly, deeply and irrevocably in love with ourself once again. This practice is a remembrance that is rooted from long before we became human and it is an ancient ritualistic power we posses from the Cosmos that allows us to embody at any moment, simply by choice.

So set your resting gaze upon the eyes of the Goddess, for she has called upon you and is ready to be seen.

The Goddess has been waiting for you and has gifted you with these words, mantras and rituals. Get ready to create a beautiful nest of love, light a candle and prepare to feed your heart in this first chapter of Goddess Prayer Poetry.

From my heart to yours, I bow to you.

- Ananda Cait

ELEVATION 1: GODDESS PRAYER POETRY

In the light of truth we express and feel from the heart.

Prayer poetry is a way to express and honour the heart in all its wisdom, love, playfulness and deep pain.

In this communication with the heart, we resound these words out into the Universe with a knowing that the energy we expel, always comes back to us in the form we most deeply desire or can learn from.

Prayer poetry is a symbol to the Goddess that we are
speaking with feeling, instead of thought.
Not from what we lack, but from what we are.
That we are willing to let the heart speak, instead of the mind.

We are willing to let truth be our guide,
show us the way to the greatest good for all,
and be a flashlight along the path to freedom,
sensuality, acceptance and towards the divine embrace of love.

So speak these words, Goddess.
Speak them with the blessing and reverence of all that you are.
Speak to the Goddess within so she can hear your longing to be seen.

Let your truth be known.
Feel these words deep within your womb.

Pour them into your veins of purity that remind us
that with the birth of new life,
comes the sacrifice of our lifeblood…

Let us honour the beauty of each maturing-cycle
that comes with being a woman
and let us walk into a new day
embracing our Goddess essence within …

IGNITING THE GODDESS WITHIN

I awaken in the early hours of morning to speak
deeply into the heart of my beloved Goddess.

As I sit and await to hear her
she is in plain sight and I feel silky
sweet words caress my cheeks in the dim
light of this quiet new day.

A softness enters my heart
and kisses my forehead
covering me with a veil
of stillness.

Ready to elevate towards
higher-ground
I envision the ever-changing coloured sky
rolling along.

Steady across the mountains down
to the red river of dreams…
I feel the current
guiding me,
aligning me,
teaching me how to release.

I trust the red river
cradling me towards
her vast ocean
where I can fully surrender here
beyond my deepest desires.

She appears within the depths
swimming with ease and comfort
smiling back at me.

She is me
and I am her.

And I dive deep into her tunnel of light
beyond the shadows of doubt.

TOGETHER AGAIN

Freedom is a vile of light
that seems to shatter the very
reality that shelters me here.

Freezing me to the ground
this fear is faceless love
and I can't tear
myself apart from it at times.

Yet I see the opportunities of a far-off land.
Will I ever reach that solace place of refuge?

It's a faceless love I don't know yet,
but so is this fear.

I am currently held in a relationship
I will never truly understand.

Into the wayward wind and rain
I venture into a place that feels so
uncomfortable & desolate
I wonder if I'll ever feel completely whole.

I don't want any other shade of sadness
and so I try to stay in the only sadness I know.

Alas, I retreat…
Only to try again another day.

I will take this great leap of faith into the wild,
witnessing a sky of majestic colours
I don't yet understand.

Unaware of my sickness I've held onto for so long
I open my palms and surrender this tired grip.

I look into the bright new
colours facing me now.
Healing and cleansing me of my past
— showing me forgiveness.

My scorned heart pulses outwardly
as I embrace an open hand
reaching out to me
As if to say,
'Trust me.'

My shaking hand reaches to the light
wrapping my essence in this place of
tranquility I've never known to exist.

But oh how I've longed for you.
Sorry I forgot to see you.
Trust you.

You were always here waiting for me
to let down my guard.

It took me many sacred nights
to call in any hope of having faith...

But something in me came alive
from the numbness
to fight for you.

It had to **kill me** to find you.

For I was the guard;
The only thing blocking us
from *being together...*

GROUNDING GODDESS

Heart-to-heart in vines
of intertwining love…
the Earth gave way to
this intrinsic meeting.

The Goddess wrapped her arms
around me and placed
her crown upon the grass
as an offering of our
ever-lasting love.

I placed my forehead upon this land:
The Queen of all integration.

Gracing her soil
and this place she calls home
the nourishment of timeless tales
kept me rooting towards her core.

A fountain of nectar began to seep
into my third eye
saving me from the familiarity of the jungle
upon which she still stands.

Once a dessert with no forgiveness
I now thrive with the succulent vanquish
and the release of all her emotional debts
placed upon humanity.

'I release you now,' she says,
'You owe me nothing.'

TANTRIC EUPHORIA

I can go anywhere I want…
But you would still miss me in your bones.

Even the smallest seed
planted in the darkest of soil
will soon rush up
into the light
to feed all that is good.

The sensuality of my sweetness
is just as dark and intense
behind these lioness eyes
of tantric euphoria.

You see it as magic, victory, control.

I know it as the *surrender*
to a fire of boundless creation.

Your most potent skies couldn't hold
the crystalline stars
of divine-reflection.
Yet the purity has risen intensely
with the longing of
your graceful smile.

I take all of these delusions
and alchemize them
from my own rich-blood
into pranic potions of love
for you to savour.

The golden hour now sets in both our eyes
freeing our souls back into
the wild where we belong.

Just long enough for us
to get a taste of
what we long for…

—— Do you remember now?

STARDUST

In the grace of the Goddess
I find liberation.

This love so deep in my stardust bones
it cradles my worst fears
back into love...

This is a love I once knew
long before I ever chose
to be here.

THE HEART ARTEMIS

Not struggling to move
or get out of this nesting saviour.

I cradle my dear heart
and ask her to forgive me
for I refused to
freely feel all of her pain.

I stroke her tenderly and watch
the blood slowly return.

I want to sit with you
forever,
my dear heart.

Let me sit with you
and honour your radiant love.

Let us remove the masks
one-by-one together
as we move
deeper into the centre.

Calling to compassion…

The Goddess and I are
brought to our knees.

The ashes are
all that is left of our separation
as we fall back into grace.

We rise scorched
from the sacred fires
to unknown skies …

Soaring in unison away from the masks and lies.

YELLOW BUTTERFLY

Treading softly
I go slow.

I rest gently in the steady flow
of this glowing cocoon.

I listen beyond me
and hear the sweetgrass singing
into a chorus of hymns
I once heard long ago…

A water-coloured dream shows me
the golden hour of my life
where the yellow butterflies
saunter over wildflowers
dancing in the
warm sunlight…

Their fluttering golden wings
all around me now …
They unthread my cocoon
where I dreamt to emerge from
and offer me a new home in the sky.

One where I can spread my wings
long into the night
expanding from this sacred place
that nourished me for so long
I feel the final connection
arising within me.

I open my own golden fluttering wings
…to dance into the sky.

Soaring through hills and mountains, I cry.

It was the yellow butterfly
that showed me this place.

This is the home my heart
sought for endlessly
in the stars.

The place where I could
let my constant need to strive
and push
and fight
… fall free to the ground
beneath me.

I set it all down now.

No need for recognition
of my new golden wings.

Only gratitude and flight.

I sink deep into the blue sky
dancing into the long hours
of the morning.

Gliding and singing
a chorus so beautiful…
It's like I've never heard music before.

It was the yellow butterfly
that showed me this place:
To BE in the essence of sensual living.

And I repeat this hymn into my golden years…
I am.
I am.
… I simply am.

And I bask in the presence that these
new glorious wings are mine…

A golden gift from a long journey home,
fondly remembered.

IN THE EVE OF SUMMER

The warm summer air
so comfortable upon my silky skin
it fills my heart with a steady glow.

Soft candied skies
reflect in my Halo of
liberation and belonging
shining an effervescent
glow from the Goddess' roots
onto this newly placed crown.

Eyes glowing into lavender
fields of a personified grace
so neatly prepared and collected.

The desert rose
calling me back home into her arms
once again…

I slip into an August memory
and an infinite moment in time.

MESSAGES

Resounding messages
offered deep in the heart of my most
vibrant dreams.

Taking me through timelines of
bright projection
like a movie scene
disconnected from the storyline
of my life.

Each fragment woven
into a patchwork
of time and space.

Glowing fluorite lights the way
into the Astral Plane
beyond the veil
of my imagination.

Cosmic secrets whispered through
the night --
I feel the Archaic rhythms
of the Raven-medicine
welcoming me
into my shadow.

My inner-child glows with glee upon my arrival
she lifts up her arms to say,
"Hold me."

Heart-to-heart we cradle
each other in violet skies that
gently fade down into the ground.

"You're ok now," I say.

"We're ok now."

INTO THE HEART OF GAIA

In my reverent place of peace
I fall deep into a longing of passionate
awakening with the Earth.

I feel the impeccable ash of her slow death.

Like the sun, she approaches me without condition
showing me the difference between life and death.

This life-force energy
inviting me to lean inwards
towards my creator…

This devotion and gratitude
feed my body
like potent water
accumulating into Prana.

Opening to her ocean of love
I call out for her reclaim
and I feel her waters rush into
my creases and cruxes of
distilled heart-connection.

I begin to trust in the
moment of orgasmic unfolding
and in the mystery of this softness.

Silently I walk through thousands of years
to find myself back here with her.

Predestined from a past life
I arrive into my awakening
charged with the task of emerging
from the Shakti temple
to birth her creation.

And finally my naked feet land upon her barren soil.

I glisten with the radiant dew of
Gaia once again.

And I blaze into the wild
touching the wounds of her sensitive soul.

I do not show up in this way to save her,
I simply ask for her reverence
and to witness my own transformation.

Alchemizing this sacred
intention into Wholeness
as the entire Universe receives
her full-bodied divine-blood.

I begin to love her back to life.

I hear the call of the rare, unique
jewels in the ancient feminine spirit.

The Earth's acclaimed sisterhood
arrives to her side with deep purpose.
Chosen to bring their
intuitive codes to her.

Correlated with the moon phases
they flock to her with their offerings.
Placing them upon her altar of humanity.

Surrendering into a
soothing conversation
as she shares celestial secrets
into our existence.

"I have medicine for you,
respectfully enter anywhere,
tread softly, ask for permission
— and all of me will receive you…"

We sink deep into her eyes
and swim into her ocean of
no beginning and no end.

Denying no river.

LILITH

This divine love is like Heaven
taking the place
of something evil.

The Garden of Eden has ended
and the woman that was told
to stay quiet now dances in the roses.

She tasted the sweet juices of
cherries and wine
now flowing from
her cellular seams.

She falls in love with the thorns,
the petals,
and its labyrinth
becomes her.

Her expansive love that once
lived in the dying grip of
another being
now washes away.

Her avowed royalty-blood
washes her clean and
grants her darkest
moments of seduction.

**She is the Queen of New Eden
finally crossing the threshold.**

*Changing the ordinary world…
and revealing her heart.*

MYSTIC RELATIONS

Expansive starry-mirrored sea
I dip my toe into your
wide rolling rhythm.

Beating to the mystic relations of
Grandmother Moon…
Honouring how deep her wisdom flows.

The revenant undertaking
pulls me off balance.

I let go of this life
I've built so perfectly
one sacred shell at a time.

I am in awe of her tide
and her conviction to soften me
To pull me in …
again and again…

I sync up with her cradling rhythms
and roll into a new dawn...

RAINBOWS

I never really noticed that
I had to decide to put on a mask
or live my own life.

Now moving out of the darkness
I finally let go of the burden
to be one of them.

An etheric being
living on the outside
never understanding the masks
that were shown to me…

I was always guided to the
sadness that provoked me
like a trance.

The only feeling
that ever felt real.

There's nothing to hold onto now.

I let go of the reins of this wild horse
and give up my search for
invisible colours.

No more chasing rainbows.

The ever-shifting colours shine
for me now in hues of grace
for the journey back home …

The sky is painted just for me
amidst the humid sunlight
showering me with treasure.

Celebrating my truth…
and shining forever.

THE ASTRAL PLANE

Tomorrow never came
and I lost myself in the battle
of its promise.

I was caught up in the dance.

But I woke up
with the answer of the stars
who took my hand
and guided me out
to the other side.

My modern manifesto
was my own journey back home
into this map of an aligned sky
deep within my heart.

Finally the moon would
share its secrets with me
honouring my awareness
of its magic.

I felt its pull and shift within me
awakening the Goddess
as she showed herself through the
convergence of lines in the distance.

The poetry poured through my blood
and casted a spell on this illusion of destiny
showing me a painting of
no boundaries,
no paths,
and no signs.

Just the astral plane
where there are dreams I've never seen…

all coming true.

GLORY TRAIN

This life
creates a door
closing the oasis of
claiming the existential
dreamer within.

I want to be the
magic I feel within
but I let this humanity
claim it for itself.

Keeping me small
scared,
and unworthy.

I gave it to them
all of them
little-by-little.

Yet these sparks of emotion
rock me so softly
it still feels so good…
like a hit to my lungs
seeping into my veins
and into the cosmic dream.

I decided to let go
into the vastness of the unknown.

Finally claiming the keys to my own glory.

My own blessing.

And then the Goddess showed me
how to fly to the moon.

DELUSION

In my hysteria
I witness my own demise.

Dizzying and quaking the ground before me…

I lay down on the sun-baked surface
and I hand over my search to be free.

I lay with breathless tears ---
The only thing cleansing
the Earth beneath me
holding this cosmic body.

I give up on reaching for answers
And call upon my faith for comfort.

"Come to me now and
take from me what I cannot comprehend.
Let me rest in your arms
for I am lost in a dry, deserted land
so vast …

I cannot see your starlit patchwork
beyond the wavering horizon."

A white cloak of light lands
around my limp body
showering me with a
blessing of truth.

"Rest my sweet child…
for my patchwork of aligned stars
lives within you."

The sun showers open around me
and I lay in this sensual healing
feeling my body come back alive
one rainbow drop at a time
softly kissing my skin.

I let go of my search to be free
and lay deep within the returning Sahara waters

gifted back unto the Earth
simply because it was asked.

And in my everlasting return to this love
I remember…

We all pray in the end.

INTERLUDE

Her.

She feels familiar.

BACK TO THE RIVER

So far from home
I lost sight of why I left
but I was in love with my future.

Under the umbrella tree
where I used to spend
summer nights by the rocky river
I dip my toes into
trickling sounds…

Bathing in these waters that baptize me
again and again.

Pondering the sweetness
of my years
I fondly play with
my complexion
in the ripples.

I witness the river.

She is my teacher.

Honouring her grace
as she lives forever.

Long into the moment.

FIRST LOVE

… And then she bounced back
out of the only love she'd ever known.

It never dawned on her to stay.

Hell had seemingly taken over and stripped her naked
cutting off her ability to feel.
Numb.
Blind.

When the blunt force trauma
pushed her under — she dove down into the waters
to find gems of revelation.

Heart neural pathways opened
a rush of succulent flavour drove through the very centre
of her sinister awakening…

And as she crawled out from the cold, unforgiving river
she landed onto the soft moss of Heaven…

Emerald green light now radiates from the very space that killed her.

… yes.

The very space that saved her.

THE BECKONING

A ritual of gardens and light-works
that severs me so deeply into the
sweetness of my very breath, I ask...

"Where is the Goddess I so truly desire?
Are you really there?
Or are you only a fragment of time
so exquisitely thrown out of context?"

I open my heart now and a gust
of freedom adorns my chest
lifting me up and shadowing my doubts
tossing them into the fire
never to be felt again
embraced by the deepest
acceptance I've ever known.

I see you — Yes.

I feel you — Yes, my love.

And the liberation sinks in like
a deeply seeded desire
finally quenched of its thirst...

beckoning into my soul.

HE RISES TO MEET HER

'Worship me,' my heart says.

The sky plays to
an unsung song
but it wouldn't last long.

Time slows down as
daisies bloom.
I wait for no-one
to taste my perfume.

***He rises to
partake in
the heaven I create.***

Dripping down to his tongue…
— the connection finally sung.

He can't escape
my sweet affection
as he rises to meet me
between our reflection.

Out here in the daisies…

He greets an obsession
and tears out his heart
with every confession.

PERSEPHONE

And the sun rushed out of tantric skies
leaving her to be alone
with the night.

She fell from the moment of grace
and into the painful grip of the Underworld
where soon she would become Queen.

She gasped in the night
before the dawn lifted her up
and set her back into the stormy sea.

She swam away from the
torture where she could heal
in a soft womb to hear her Mother Demeter
comforting her.

Her rose garden dreams were set on
fire by thieves
but she took back the night
dove deep into her darkness
where she birthed fruits of her labour
and decided never again
to fall to pieces
for Hades.

She fell in love with her creator.

The divine love took her by surprise
but saved her from the
darkness that used to scare her.

She bowed to the Goddess within
and felt the roots of love
deep within her many lifetimes
of learning to trust that
she would bloom again.

The unknowing bewildered
her but this is
why she came back to life
to experience

the caress on her skin
and the scorn
of the knife
burrowed deep inside her chest…

The remembrance of bitter wind
and the sun showers
that heat up the night
off the grass where
the children used to play.

The memory saved her
and brought her back from
the depths of the Underworld
of which she had to learn to treasure.

*It is the maze
she has to walk through
each time as she resurfaces
with the gifts of the unseen.*

She was kidnapped and owned by
a jealous patriarch that never
truly appreciated her beauty.

Until now when she
blooms every spring
and brings back the scent of Heaven.

She is the seasons.
The eternal cycle of
Mother's death
and rebirth.

She sacrifices herself for our own true pleasure.
We remain patient as she returns
like an old childhood friend.

*The memory never lost
only temporarily hidden
and reborn
to seduce our senses
once again.*

SHADOW-WORK ECSTASY

***This isn't the deepest
I've ever felt …
or is it?***

I wonder what else can help heal this sick wound
of insecurity within me
as I wait for the answer
from the Goddess who holds me.

I feel this pain inside my ribs
like a scathing, scabbing wound
so raw and vulnerable that the slightest
touch will trigger me into
an emotional storm of chaos.

I hold my sweet heart and ribcage
and promise my inner child
that no matter what I'll be there by her side.

But the scathing pain persists
and I am trapped in the moment
only to feel the Universe's
relentless push to reawaken me from within.

It's the most pain I've ever felt.

To be so alone
so raw
so vulnerable
and I feel like I can't trust
anyone, but myself.

The Universe holds me here
like I'm gazing into a
mirror of horrors.

All the things that embarrass me
that make me feel less than…
and all the ways the world
could hurt me so deeply.

I feel so empty
so lost.

Yet I hold my wound inside my ribs
knowing that this will
pass if I just sit and feel it all.

If I can just breathe and hum
and let this be birthed through me like a baby
trying to escape its Mother's womb.

Tearing and scarring my insides
like an emotional knife that makes me
never want to see my beloved face again.

It all comes back to this child that feels lost.

She examines her truth and knows that
she cannot escape the past
she can only embrace it
heal it
cradle it
and mourn it.

It's a savoury place to be at times
yet this time all I want to do is make it end
'make the pain stop!'
I scream inside my heart.

But yet it persists
expanding time…
I couldn't fathom
or see it clearly.

Just pain…
sweet pain…
coursing though a vortex
in my heart.

And then the darkness falls away suddenly
and a warm numbness
enters into my ribs
echoing into the darkness
….a sense of comfort.

I let go into the night
and surrender this pain to my angels
for they seem to know what I need.
I try my best and
wait for the night to pass.

In the daylight of my youth
I reawaken to feel once again
what makes me feel
so connected to my heart.

It's a place I've lived in before
yet the shadow-work puts me back into
this humble union with the cosmic cutting.

I am nothing compared to what I have to learn.
And all I feel is this longing to be ok again.

So I sit and feel the tension behind my ears
break into a thousand needles penetrating my brain
and the loud shriek of a cry
enters the room
as if my child has died
and I don't know myself anymore.

Her need to be seen has gone away…
and all I feel is an empty space
ready to be filled by something new.
Something lighter
a smile
a nap
a nest.

And I learn to seep deep into the wisdom
of this great awakening once again.
Learning to stop the judgement of my own demise
for I have died a thousand times …

But I always come back to life.

I am reborn into this channel of light
and connected to the heart of
this never-ending awakening.

SELF-WORSHIP

The Goddess chooses me as her muse.
Her Shakti Serpent ready to rise
with thirsty teeth
spellbound by tantric potions.

Her intuitive knowing
sent to me in a love note
so sweet to the taste of consideration.

She tells me to read every word out loud.
Serenading myself in her poetic seduction.

She begins to caress my vessel
down to my naval
to my outpouring vortex of nectar.

Teaching me how to make love to myself.

How to make Love with God.

In this newly discovered relationship
I am finally set free to swim
in my own flowing essence
without apology.

I wash her blessed waters upon my skin
and feel her ever-sensual drip
covering me from my lips
down my nipples
and into my naval.

Trickling past my legs
and rooting in-between my curling toes …

I taste the nectar
that makes me quiver
into the coursing river rushing
through my body.

I begin to understand what it feels
like to be ravished
and loved obsessively.

To be worshipped.

I break away from the
fear of being abandoned
and I enter Heaven here…
within myself…
in this touch…

My soft fingertips trace
the surface of stars upon my skin
slowly down my throat and
over my collarbones …

Diving into my heart chakra here
to honour my own ecstatic love.

It's like falling in love for the first time
and quenching the aching need
for my own attention.

Like an angel's kiss of heroin
rushing though my veins and
opening the windows of
my soul…
released into a sky of infinite stars.

***Any guilt is now purified with
expanded Universal love
adorning me.***

Washing through me…

With the pulsing of my womb in a cosmic climax
my heart breaks open with a wave of emotion
seeping from my eyes….
and cleansing my aura.

Sending a gasp of air into the room.

EMBROIDERED LANGUAGE

The new beginning is a prevalent evolution.

Unraveling the most
basic human emotions.

I let go of the need to
constantly control,
rescue and distrust my future.

This consistent storyline in my mind
for perfectionism must be healed.

For the long road up
ahead will never be travelled
if I do not learn to set myself free
within the discomfort of
transformation.

The road that presents itself to me
towards the horizon of freedom
has long meant for me to travel.

It has called to me
beyond the trees
where I chose to lose
my intuition and direction.

But there it is
clearly paved to
perfection.

I see it now and its open sky.
It grants me access to a well-lived life
beyond the corridors of my own setting sun.

NOSTALGIC WATERS

These waters bless my
tired soul as it refuses to die…
I transform and alchemize
into the depths of these waters
I feel so deeply within my heart.

This desire to go back.

Not to the people
or to the past…
but to the feeling the moment possessed.

Safe, unscathed, innocent.

But my pure inner light of awareness knows
it can never be bruised.

It existed long before it entered this body
and will live long after
this blessed vessel
has been synched as a channel.

The memories, however…
they still fill up my storybooks of scripture
that once were read, lived and turned over.

Some fondly and deeply remembered;
others burned.

But the book of my life
is colourful…

and I wouldn't have it any other way.

NEW EDEN

The Goddess walks with rose pedals
and starlit footprints …

She leaves a path
where all her sisters may find her
at the edge of nowhere.

She knows that when they reach her
it will be to the risk
of their own demise…

She has heard the cry of their
bruised and beaten hearts
burned and broken
again and again.

Yet it is HER heart
that is a reflection of them all.

The very gateway to the un-shattering
of crystalline mirrors
showing them the way
through the dark forest of stars
and wilted roses…

And so they walk through the vortex
hand-in-hand…

with profound unity.

ALIVE AGAIN

I dreamt
about that dopamine hit
I gave away
again and again…

The drugs weren't there anymore
and I died in the arms of a mortal trance.

I gave him all I had.
He died, yet stayed.
Looking for fun and getting high for free.

The rumbling from distant shores
rocked me to sleep.
Her shallow call was
a deep knowing that
was inevitable like moon medicine.

He said I need to stop feeling so much …

But the Mother broke the shackles.
She saw I was dead.
A shell of nothing.
I prayed for her to save me.

She had me roll naked into her soil of diamonds.

I felt my pulse getting louder
as she stripped me down
and sang songs to the beat of my heart…
Then drove me deep into her waters.

"Lean into me," she committed.

And I found the courage to cry with the Mother
as she avowed her love for me;
No one can hold me like her.

MUSHROOM FOREST

I call in magic from the forest.

Living amongst the big trees…
It was the Redwoods that called me here.

The hymn of her friends so glorious
in the trees of magic.

Her existence is potent forest medicine.

She gifts me magic
mushrooms into the wild.

Her tiny forest messengers
listen to all the secrets whispering
amongst her soil and transmute her stories
to others across her palace…

She is the power to cure.

The extracts
that shield
my body.

Never to experience sickness again
I trust in this Utopian circle of her Divine sustenance.

DIVINE ALIGNMENT

I Speak to her
I pray to her
and I feel her in my body.

If the answer is yes when my
feet are planted into her Earth…

Then I allow her message to guide me.

This is my journey.
This is my intuition.

I trust in me…
and all my glorious
wisdom.

ELEVATION 2:
GODDESS MANTRA

Mantra is the art of speaking to our inner Goddess with love to awaken her into a healthier lifestyle: one where we are our own loving parent.

Have you ever spoken to your inner-child? Is she weeping inside without anyone who can support her and tell her she is ok now? It's so important to remind our subconscious mind that where we are now is safe, loving and that any trauma from the past is now over. Our inner-child tends to stay in the past, holding onto all the pain. She pushes this trauma to the forefront by dictating decisions from a place fear, but the Goddess realizes there is nothing to be fearful of that once lived in the past. She is a Mother to the inner-child and always speaks from a place of love and support.

This is why speaking proactive words to ourself with love is so important. We must remind ourselves that we are beautiful, worthy and of value simply for being alive.

There are simple affirmations that can be used to build up our love muscles in the mind and in the heart. Once these affirmations are used day-after-day, we can become stronger and create a loving relationship with ourselves that ultimately will reflect in how we approach the world as well. The mind has a pattern it will go back to if the pattern is strong. This means the thought process we choose regularly is the strongest one we've chosen to feed throughout our entire lifetime thus far.

You can think of these muscles as fear-based muscles and love-based muscles. Notice which thought comes up first for you about a specific decision. Do you trust yourself to move forward or, do you tell yourself you're not worthy or capable to make the decision? Without judgement, we must choose again. In order to call in the Goddess, we must choose love over fear. We must forgive our fears and hand them over to the Cosmos.

To do this, mantras and affirmations are a very powerful and mystic tool that can completely re-wire our subconscious minds and heal our inner-child, simply by paying more attention to our thought-process and halting it when we want the Goddess to lead the way.

Is this to say we should never be fearful or have an ego? Absolutely not. There will always be a place for our ego in order to survive, but if you have picked up this book you know there is more to life than just survival. There is an ease to life that is waiting for you to tap into it and say, 'yes'.

The ego is fruitful soil from which the holy spirit can work upon. This means that if we had no drive to get ahead or share something with the world, nothing would be created. The ego wants to be put to work, however the work must be driven from inspiration, not expectation. This is how we know who is in the drivers seat of our life. The ego — or the Goddess (Source)? The ultimate truth is to listen to what excites us about life, then use the ego to push our dreams out into the world. But the ego has a place, it cannot be driving the car and when it hides like sugar in our mind through the need for recognition, approval, judgement and comparison of others, we ultimately know to fall into softness once again and listen to our inner Goddess.

We have the power to consciously tell the ego to rest from time-to-time through the conscious act of mantra and affirmation. This is the most potent potion and spell to cast control over our wandering fears.

What do all these themes between source and ego have in common; balance. Balance is the key to ultimately letting the Goddess thrive and flow with the river of life. We do not want to fall into the delusion of making our ego our enemy, but simply to work with it and be its parent. The Goddess knows when to nourish the ego as well as when to discipline it. It is a conscious dance that becomes playful with time and experience.

Throughout this chapter, you will find mantras that allow you to move through some of the darker times when the ego has taken hold of your heart. These mantras have been transcended and alchemized from the

Goddess to provide an awakening into your higher-self. Once the inner-child is calm and happy, you will begin to tap into the true beauty of life.

You will begin to notice the loving signs from the Universe telling you that you're on the right path forward as you begin to collaborate with the Cosmos. It is in co-creation with the Universe where the Goddess is at her ultimate best. She allows the signs to guide her and she acts accordingly, feeling the passion for these signs along the way and she stays conscious to the signs of discomfort that guide her back towards love as she begins to set healthy boundaries with the world because she loves and respects herself.

Through the art of mantra you can speak to your heart and remind yourself of what is healthy and loving. The Goddess has a deep intrinsic loving relationship with herself and she knows who she is because she has loved herself into her own personal Heaven. Are you ready to create this loving relationship with yourself and call in the Goddess?

The mantras in this chapter are alchemized, meaning they are more euphoric than most mantras you would find. I suggest you circle or highlight certain lines within these poetic mantras that resonate with your heart. This way you can write them out and paste them somewhere where you will always see them. Some of you may also feel called to write out an entire mantra poem and frame it on the wall if it resonates with you deeply.

These mantras are an offering of love from the Goddess and the Cosmos. They have been preciously gifted to me to share with the world, knowing that those who read them are meant to have them. They were transcended for you and so I know they will resonate in some way, whether it's today or sometime in the future.

I want to thank the Universe for gifting us with these gems of realization in order to speak to our inner-child and call in the Goddess from within. We know she is waiting for us to call upon her through our acts of loving kindness towards ourselves.

It all comes down to the sound of our own personal love song. Enjoy and drink in every word, sweet Goddess. Let's begin with a love note to the Universe.

LOVE NOTE TO THE UNIVERSE

GODDESS within;

The beginning of something entirely new is upon me now and I am guided to a new level of seeing and being heard.

Only you know of the true path I am to wander.

Stepping back, I let go of everything I know I cannot control.

May I be guided to the highest action of
love and truth in the midst of my soul's revolution.

In truth and reverence, I will sit and listen to your messages now.

GODDESS:

Dear one,

You are a beautiful being beyond measure and your
tenacity for life is to be admired.

This is a beautiful time for you and the journey within will always be the best part of your life.

You know of this and are aware, but please try not to control your process…It's all being taken care of by the highest supported energy.

I know what you need and what your prayers are;
for I am here in the dark with you too, always listening.

Do not be sad, dear love.
It will all work out the way it must.
You are a light-worker and this is your calling.

Follow the light, Goddess.
You will find it when it hits you.

Yours Truly,
Universal Love.

PRESENT REFLECTION

In-tune with this life.
I am balanced, healthy and happy.

I live day-to-day.
Joyful in the life I've created.

Genuine sisterhood
is pulled to my heart.

Sweet fruit.
Flowers.
Sun showers.
Life.

All is well in this moment.

INTERLUDE

I trust fully in the process of life to take care of me.
I will not be angry with myself or others —
For this is not needed
along the path of transformation.

Today… I will make patience a priority
for myself and others along the way.

Compassion is my greatest ally.

LIBRA LOVE

I am the colour
of deep gorgeous fuchsia pink
that wraps around everything
and everyone I so deeply love.

I am the rose that shines under
the light of Venus in a dark field.

I am the Goddess that reminds you how
good it feels to be alive. Like a succulent sun shower
in a rain forest of electric
thunderstorms approaching.

My beauty shines so bright that it might
seem dangerous
to some…

I am alluring and bewitching
and they miss me most of all…

In the golden hour
I make ordinary moments magic
and manifest my every single hope
away from the kingdom of tragic.

With feathered wings I take flight
up and up into the distance
beyond your pure sight.

I am the tree of life
and the sweet fig.

The bounty of sweet fruit
you are free to admire…

But beware with your desire.

Behind these sweet eyes
there is a dark angel
in disguise

Who will love you without compromise.

GODDESS ISIS

Laying my armour down,
I fall neatly into her arms.

"You are everything… don't you see?"
She says while tracing stars
around my scars.

Rising up from the mist
I see the sun born again in her eyes.

Her warmth shines upon my face
and sparks a benevolent fire
soaring through my chest.

Eyes of gold open
I gleam into her wildest desire
to set the entire Universe on fire.

In awe of her ineffable wonder
I feel her loving touch
reminding me
this is a place of
certain transformation.

The sun will set --- Yes.
But the sun will also rise again.
It will take me out of this painful night.

She meets me at the Altar
as I fall to my knees…

And the stars impregnate me…

With the birth of a brand new day.

I AM ENOUGH

Is it enough to simply be
to breathe
to sit here with the pain.

It is enough to cry
and surrender these burdens
You have chosen to carry.

It is enough to fall down
and fail completely.

But remember sweet Goddess...

It is also enough to allow a sweet embrace
To call out for help
When you crumble into sand

It's enough to surrender completely
let the waves mangle you
To feel their humbling wrath
And draw you back into a sea of recalibration

It's enough to feel the death of a beautiful rose…
so two new ones have the chance to finally open

And so I ask you…

Let down your guard
and let the healing begin.

For it's enough to let your wounds
bleed & cleanse

To let them Pulse
while you comfort them.

For the stars are always in alignment

And our seasons still remain.

And so we pray.

CONNECTION TO SELF

I release into my breath now…

Willing to feel my body
Willing to feel the rising up
of my emotions
I've long neglected.

The waves rise and fall in my chest
as I hold space …
simply to allow.

These waves of breath slowly
dissolve barriers to sweet
forgiveness within my heart.

Healing me from what I cannot see
My Kriyas twitch and move
in flowing, minute
storms throughout my body.

The waves rise and crash in my chest
as I continue to hold space …
Simply to allow.

The grace of the Goddess
holds me here.

She is a reflection
of my pure inner light of awareness…

My Purusa.

Never born, never died.

And I become one with her…
The connection bonds us
in a vortex of sweeping realities
lost in a playbook
of shattered illusions.

Holding hands
we set the sails of faith

Into one another
porting out into the wild seas.

We brace the storm...
waves rushing and crashing
over our bonded bodies
faster and more powerful than ever before.
Cracking my heart open
with each ego-death.

Collecting bodies of feminine water
I sit in worship of this earth-rooting humility
my Dharma swallows me whole
and there is no going back now.

The waves rise up this time
to lift us towards our destiny together
and we take back the love
we've remembered for so long.

The waves now falling
into a silent sphere of resonance
along a steady horizon within …

A reflection of a starlight ritual
now dances upon these tranquil waters
mirrored into a clear blue sky.

I am so grateful for us
as I hold space here
simply to allow…

A CALL FOR PEACE

Sitting in this place of power
The entire world meets me
in its breath and presence.

I sync to the channel of transcendence.

A guiding voice welcomes me into the mantra
with playful sincerity
Om, my heart...

The Gayatri gleams with each rocking cradle
like a deep ecstatic trance.

Chanting with the rhythm of our teachers
I feel the pulse of our voices
gleaming in time
across the world together.

Holding our Earth in the tranquil
blue spirit of peace
my tears of gratitude sweep me
back into an ocean of bliss.

Jai Jai Guru Dev
Prånama.

In dedication to my teachers, Deva Premal and Miten.
Thank you for your daily grace.

SILENT IN THE STARS

Seeking nothing
I go inwards…

Sick with despair
I find a place of solace
In the silence between my eyes.

LOVING INTUITION

A mantra to build trust with intuition.

A crashing of instinct
rushes from my naval
and into my conscious heart.

I listen with reverence and pray
this trust won't give out.

Like a beckoning from heaven
saying, 'don't let this happen'
I free myself with the
Ultimate Casting.

'No,' I declare with love and free aim
'This heart is no place
for you to pour your sweet pain.'

And I stake my own claim
along my heart-Earth plane
screaming inside
with the new freedom
to be me…

'Let love live here now
and resound with the infinite stars
waiting for me to be seen,'

Their sweet alignment
always written in the sky
long before I've lived and died.

'I trust you great spirit within
let us dance together
along my path of glistening stars…

Lead me beyond what I currently know
and show me self-trust
the further I go…'

HEALING

I must learn to hold this pain
if I am to change.

If I can learn to hold this pain
and sit with it
ask it questions
be aware of what it means
understand where it lives within my body…

I know that I can heal
and dial into my higher-self.

This feeling of emotional pain is what
will ultimately change and heal me.

I know that holding pain
is necessary for change
and I am strong enough to hold myself
in this space where this pain needs to be felt
embraced, honoured and then released.

I am also aware that I can still
experience joy in the presence of pain.
I can feel more than one emotion
at a time and this is what makes
life so amazing.

I am the Universe coming to life
to simply experience itself and
transcend all the glory that exists
here in the dream of the mind.

A sacrifice must be made to heal
and I am willing to go deep
into the heart of this pain

***look it straight in the eye
and ask
'What do you need from me?'***

ISVARA

I am a lighthouse
with the opening channel for Source.

Source has chosen me to be of service
to those that would have me speak to them
and hear the message from how I perceive life.

The Universe has planted a seed
within my heart that has gifted
me the freedom to nourish
and grow an abundant garden of my own.

The garden will be open to all who choose
to bask in its beauty and wisdom.

May they take what they need
and I will acknowledge that even
if the message is not received or not meant
to resonate now…
it was always meant to be for them.

And the fruits of this playful meeting will
resound later into this life
and long into the next.

For their spirit and mine
were always meant to meet
and reinforce the intelligence of *Isvara:*

The all-encompassing
pool of knowledge.

EGYPTIAN FLOW

In the rivers of Babylon
We bathed in way-showers

Noticing…
This body-connection to pleasure…

We washed in the
healing reflection of the sky
Exploring these colourful vessels.

Cleansing painful memories
of the times we once were
touched without reverence.

Surrendering to the slow sensation.

At times orgasmic.

The liberation disarms us
with profound intention
and opens us to
integration.

GRANDMOTHER MOON

Grandmother moon
you have a permanent
and deep-rooted courtship
with the Goddess.

Their wounds shift and reflect in each others
patterns within the sky.

Divine Feminine wisdom
signifies intuition
like a treasure map towards union and peace.

Grandmother moon
you travel through my dreams
and awaken parts of myself so desperate to be seen
it feels foreign at times when my Goddess
finally awakens into the spotlight
of your light.

The darkness of you symbolizes
my need to go inwards
and create a nest where I can be lost
in an ocean of tears.

I release into the night and know that
you are my teacher
moulding me into
my higher-self.

You are the grandmother of us all
and you know best in all your shapes
and travels. You reach into my blood
and create waves of sweet emotion
that last long into the golden years of my life.

Oh Grandmother moon,
how you have always been here for me
teaching me, loving me,
and truly knowing me.
—Thank you.

THE OWL HUMS

Sweet sundown
the white owl hums.

I listen with a heart-centred gaze
as she sits in stillness.

Sweet sundown
the white owl hums.

Her deep eyes
reflect in the drums.

A calm purring of
wisdom permeates like
moon beams on hillsides.

The white owl hums
A wisdom so fine…

So honest and baring
it seeks for me to see.

SOUL STAR SISTER

I see you Goddess as you stare back at me.

No walls to shake this gaze
no sense of being untold.

I see you
your grace
and my compassion unfolds.

The offerings you bring me
penetrates into the dark.

The wisdom I see
the graceful step in your spark.
—-
I feel open and free here
no need to make a remark.

A sparkle in these tears
that wash over me now.

I feel so much for you
and I bow.

I feel the building reverence
for your presence and mine…

On this Earth together at the same time…

So we may witness
each other glowing
long into the dawn.

Oh, what a miracle this is…
we've met in this lifetime
and many beyond.

ELEVATION 2.1: INNER-CHILD HEALING

The inner-child is a long forgotten part of who we are. The experiences we receive as a child live long and deeply rooted into our subconscious mind of the inner child, refusing to let go of the pain they once endured. More than this, the inner-child also holds on to great joy and ecstatic freedom of experiences because it is the part of us that was taking-in feelings for the very first time.

When we experience anything for the very first time it's a potent moment. Our subconscious mind takes it in and however it resonated with us tends to dictate our decisions in the future. Either to recreate a moment that was joyful and euphoric or to stay away from experiences that caused us deep pain.

The inner-child does not come out to play unless it is nurtured, adored and disciplined by its adult-self. It lives in the background of our minds and in the deep neural pathways of our energetic heart-system. Our fears generally rely fully on our inner-child perception of the world around us and unless it is given time and space to be nurtured, it will never let go of this fear to survive.

The feeling of diving into the inner-child energy is usually quite painful when we are willing to look at how we have not become the parent or support system we've needed all these years. However, the inner-child when set free to play, comes alive and feels free to express her deepest desires as well as her fears.

Creating a safe *Goddess Nest* to play, dance, sing, paint or just be silly is an incredible healing space where your inner-child can come forward and show herself to you if you allow her to and listen with your heart. The most important part of this process is to truly accept whatever comes up from your inner-child without judgement and with forgiveness of the many fears it has held onto for so long. Let the Goddess step forward and become the parent of your inner-child.

Your higher-self is the greatest parent we have long awaited—we are all looking for a place to feel like we belong and are at home. Some would say we spend our entire lives looking for a place where we can feel at home once again (to fit in), but when the inner-child is fully seen, nurtured and protected… she will no longer search for a place outside of herself to call home. She will be at home within the arms of your loving care and unconditional support and here, she can finally rest.

To begin the process of healing and creating a bond with our inner-child we must learn to create time and space for connection.

The *Goddess Nest* is a way to feel safety in the touch of your tender emotional wounds and to draw-out your vulnerabilities and realize that they are the most beautiful part of who you are. It is a miracle to be triggered and to feel raw and vulnerable because this is where we can pinpoint the exact place of our needed healing. This also means that the Universe has made it clear that we are ready to heal this part of ourself.

There are parts of you that you may not even realize are still there, that you may have consciously worked through or thought you let go of. But the reality of our emotions is that they stay buried deep inside until we are ready to feel all their pain and recognize what has been living deep within. Most of us shy away from this type of deep work because emotions of shame, guilt, distrust and anger are not embraced within society.

My hope for you is that you recognize when you sit in deep silence, your intuition will rise and you will be able to create a deep bond within. This bond will soon be a familiar place called home and you will feel safe in the company of oneness.

It's time to release what no longer serves you and get in touch with your child within. She has waited so long to feel your love and forgiveness. Talk to her, embrace her, play with her and let her know you are here for her.

MY INNER-CHILD

I see you sitting there across
the room in the corner…

Your head hangs down as
you turn to me with
broken eyes.

'It was one night that made you feel unsafe
when no one told you, you would be ok.'

I reach out my hand as she looks up to me
with hesitant belonging…

I grab her hand and pull her into me
with a heart beaming full of love and comfort
that we've finally found each other.

'I am your Mother now,' I remind her.
'I'll never let you go nor will I let you get hurt.'

And I can feel her arms grip around me
a bit tighter as if she's been saved
from the perfect storm…
waiting in the sea of waves
with no-one to turn-to.

Her heart beats faster
but this time with the reminder
of the freedom to let go
of the fear she's been
carrying for all these years.

'The story is not real,' I remind her,
'It's not for us anymore.'

I caress her head and her hair
in this loving embrace to unfold
and unwind.

I can feel her heart loosening
and opening up with the
assurance of a new day.

'I'm here now and no one can hurt you,' I whisper
as we hold onto each other long
into the night in a nurturing cradling rhythm.

Tears fall from my eyes as an
opening in my heart becomes clear.

'This is home now,' I reclaim,
'the place where we can rest.'

MY JOURNAL

You hold all my secrets
and heart epiphanies that
once seemed so distant from me.

I look back now and see a
girl who was learning to grieve
and grow strong.

Through her reflections
she religiously showed up for herself
and grew up into the parent
she always longed for.

The lover she always fought for.

The friend she never betrayed.

She became it all.

And throughout the years of reflection
she finally became herself.

THE WAY

Let the way of the heart
shine through.

I am but a reflection of the
musical beating drum of my life.
And my recognition of this unity
calls in one eternal heart.

Love upon love
we shine into the dark.

The Universal heart pulses
me into a divine
balance of freedom.

All the darkness disappears into one
as I let the way of the heart shine
past the line of separation.

I let love reign
and the entire world beats as one.

Light upon light.
Hand upon heart.
Eyes upon source…

My divine light embraces
a new way forward…

I fade into one ocean
and let the way of the heart
guide me towards salvation.

BLUE FIRE

The Goddess lit the fire…
trusting the flickering flame
dancing in the wind
that carries it without
setting the Earth ablaze.

It holds me here deep
in a daze
of sleep and awake.

A violet wave travels through coals
and caves so deep
rooting me down
where I lay and entice a trance
awakening and preparing
my soul to receive such treasures.

I feel the life-blood coiling
around my neck
as I reassess the truth
and the wisdom of the fire.

This is a truth I've remembered
so many times before.

In the softness of these sacred sheets
that lay across my naked body.
The wind carries over me
hugging me here solid to the ground.

The primal fire and wind feed their
aching need to burn through
my tightly wound ropes
adorned beneath my chest.

I am held in this tucked away
stillness to burn and ravage …
into a rebellious love.

Steadily whole within myself.

My spine is the fountain
as I let my heart engage in the pulse of
the acceptance of all that I do not know.

I release into the flame
and this season
of reflection.

I awaken into the night to reclaim
my direction.

It dims into ashes
back into the night.

Already truth.
Already light.

Maybe she's right…
I do not need to fight.

I AM

'I am but I am', she said.

' I walk the
path one step at a time
towards my own reflection.'

I SURRENDER NOW

Angels please arrive and meet me here
in the white golden light.

Hear me from my heart
and know that my truth
is written for you to read.

I wish to be honest
and let go of this place
I cannot interpret.

Let me release the
struggle for answers
and claim peace
with your guidance
now and forever.

I release this to you now
into the Cosmos
to foster and release
back to me when
I can taste your every sweet
drop of truth with reverence
to soothe this sweet pain.

I BELIEVE IN TRUE LOVE

My cradling heart
sobbing in grace pulsing into the
autumn of a new death.

Letting go of the drowning
I take my first breath.

Choosing to open even more
to the world of glory than
once before.

The fairytales I once read
now become an open door.

My heart smiles at love
in the garden and at the altar
where I drop to my knees
to know my fate and never falter.

I celebrate new beginnings
for those that have walked together.
Falling into a space
where they can lay and tether.

I see the good in this life
where love stands tall.

I smile and say yes,
for I am it all.

COMPASSION IS TRUTH

Compassion is the truth
I set free when I am
able to let go of my
need to be right.

I listen with acceptance
and not hold on so tight.

It's difficult to understand
why my way or your way
doesn't matter
when one of us says
sorry and both can forgive.

Even in the darkest of truths
— We both freely live and can let live.

THE PRACTICING PRIESTESS

The epic duo of conformity
replaces my need to ignite your flame.

It perpetually hastened
my glory and flight.

The ending was the same all along
no matter how hard I thought
I could change the minds of so many.

Yet, now I sit with the knowing
that their sight of my crown is
a reflection of ones-self.

It is a part of them
they may have chosen to deny
or accept with grace.

But with this recognition…
I send them love
by embodying my truth
and shining. before them.

I rope my intellect
to my actions in this life.

Not only a student
but tapped into a channel of light
where an offering from
the heart can be birthed
and awaken others into their own right.

A deep knowing from the Goddess of love.

I pray one day
they too shall become.

Where we can finally dance together
safe and soundly in the pleasure of love.

SELF-WORTH

Noble worth…
I want you to know two things:

There is no shame
in the deep desire to soar
and
there is no shame
in the deep desire to rest.

TRUE LOVE SAYS

True love says,
"I want all your phases"…

It is
the all-accepting
surrender to what is
within each other.

Its gaze and desire
never breaks;
it builds.

True love says,
"I want all your phases."

And when the dark arrives
again and again
true love says,

"I worship your raw heart,
it is but a reflection of my own."

And both loves
dive deep into darkness
together and alone.

Thanking each other each time
they can sink and bind.
Sink and bind.
Sink and bind.

True love says,
" I want all your phases."

THE FALLING STARS

The Goddess shines from within
but I see her in the sky each night.

She watches over me.
I remind her of others that
shined their light.

They were more connected
to her deep in the sky.

I feel the need to
watch the dance as I wave goodbye.

Hoping not to lose them
we hold onto their light as they go.
They belong up there with her now.

Not moving fast
Not moving slow…

Wondering where we came from…
Maybe now I know.

I wonder what life would be like without the stars…

I see a one fall …
it shifts between Saturn and Mars.

Wait don't go…
I'm glad I caught a glimpse of you.

Maybe one day I can glide and stream;
awakening the Earth too.

I FEEL HER HERE

I dance in the garden
while the wind-chimes sing.

Moving slowly
I float to the music of a warm breeze.

I live in her dream
where I can relax as I please.

The Universe tells me never to rush …
I don't need to anymore.
Leaving the past behind…
there's nothing here for me from before.

I get to be in the magic of softness
and all the comfort of the Earth.
And when the air goes still
I feel a new birth.

My Goddess shines now
after I broke down long ago
and prayed to feel fate…

Here I am
with every scene
I once hoped for:
I know it's not too late.

I have been gifted with this dance
in a place that was once beyond my vision.

The Earth goes quiet
and the air goes still
and I feel her more now
then I ever will…

MOTHER MEDICINE

Watching and observing.

Feeling into the moment.

I begin to listen.

I relax into her wisdom.

Satisfied with her experience.

I learn and grow from potent medicines.

I refuse to stay asleep.

The codes are written in the flow of the Earth.

She brings silence to my violent truth.

She deepens my connection…

I graciously receive all of her.

I stay curious in my journey home.

Merging with Magic Mother.

She has guided me here…

A part of it all.

GODDESS KALI

I let go as I fall into intrinsic realms
consecrating with dreams
I play with in the night.

I awake to Goddess Kali
with her sword to unbound me.

With her force of creation
she radiates respect.

She battles the secrets I've kept
and opens my eyes to self-inflicted pain.

I never respected this heart
enough to walk away
and so I ask…

'Goddess Kali,
release the binds I have with others
that never reflected back to me
my profound
worthiness and dignity.'

'No need to beg for love, my dear.
You are my fierce love,' she claims.

I have ignored my own deep desire to
cut this need to salvage scraps…

'NO.' She says as she slashes the chords
bound to a-thousand takers.
'Get up off the floor.'

She lays me down upon her thrown
and proceeds to tell me an unyielding truth.

'When you are devoted to your own acclaim…
you will call-in the seeker who worships and soothes.'

ELEVATION 3:
GODDESS RITUAL

Welcome to the ritual portion of this sacred book, Goddess. If you have been a practicing Goddess for a while, you will know the power of playing sincerely with ritual and ceremony.

Ritual is a powerful way to communicate to the Goddess by blessing yourself and honouring your heart-mind connection.

Ritual is not a worshiping of an energy that lives outside of you, it already lives within you and we are all able to embody this truth if we are willing to make time for it.

Creating ritual embodies the act of dreaming and bringing these symbols that resemble your dreams or feelings to a sacred altar. This becomes the tangible reflection of your heart here on Earth. So, what is an altar space?

An altar space is a place within your home or an area you've set up to create ceremony. It holds all your deepest feelings through high-vibration elements and is a way to communicate to the Goddess and the Universe that you are grateful to have the opportunity to enjoy all of life's simple gifts, while holding intention to heal and celebrate life. In this book, we will refer to the altar space as our *Goddess Nest,* which we will create around us as we gift our hearts with the amorous love we so deeply deserve.

Let's create a nest around us that holds items resembling our deepest intentions for the moment and for the future.

These items can also resemble intentions that heal the past or symbolize the letting go of emotions that no longer serve us.

Crystals can be placed with intention depending on which crystal you are guided-to. For example. rose quartz resembles the Divine Mother within and the ability to love yourself deeply. You can use this crystal as a tool to hold your Nest in divine, unconditional love.

I love to create my *Goddess Nest* with cozy blankets, pillows, scented candles, photos of my ancestors, incense, as well as essential oils and sage to clean the energy of the altar space. I love to surround my *Goddess Nest* with selenite, which is a salt crystal that amplifies high-frequency energy. Soothing music is also a beautiful way to soften deeply into your *Goddess Nest* almost immediately, either in a bath, nourishing outside in a garden or privately in your own home.

The best part of this type of ceremony is that your Nest will be personalized to you. Everything that you love will be surrounding you and mirroring your elevated essence back to you so you can amplify your auric-field. Here you can rest, dance, cry, pray, write, dream, sing, meditate, paint, yoni-steam, cover yourself with oils and flower petals as you read or just surrender to a nice long nap.

This is how the Goddess nourishes her heart and places the crown upon her head, once again.

Ritual can also include creating spell-jars to manifest intentions for yourself and others. We will discover this type of witchcraft together —- however the Goddess only engages in spell-work and ritual with the intention of transcending the greatest good for everyone involved.

The Goddess calls upon her angels of the highest truth, love and compassion when casting spells and rituals for herself and others. Universal healing golden white light will surround her as she calls upon it: conducting each ritual with deep intention of the heart, fully-protected and guided to the highest frequency of supported energy. This is how she becomes a channel of light. The Goddess views ceremony as an act of humble service to herself and the world.

Keep in mind that dark-magic and ritual does exist, however the Goddess does not view this as conducive to her or society as it usually will focus on revenge, jealousy and resentment. Dark-magic does not heal the Goddess, mainly because it focuses on problems and not solutions. So here in *The Goddess Nest* we will focus on being a channel for source, letting go of our egos, all while diving into our shadows (the subconscious-mind) to heal our darkness and conduct genuine respect for our conscious elevation.

When we focus on becoming aware and healing our own insecurities or triggers with a sense of compassion for all — we can then truly embrace all of who we are and elevate into our highest-version of The Goddess within. Let love lead the way.

To begin with each ritual, start by reading the ritualistic poetry to carry your feelings with you into the moment. Then conduct the ritual with the guidance provided here to support you.

GODDESS BLESSING RITUAL

The Goddesses spin in a circle.
Cloaked in thin white linen that flows
over their temples of light.

Candlelight dances on the walls around them
as they chant to the drum of a heavy rain.

Tall wooden pillars stand tall like ancestors
shielding the night.

Gleeful sisterhood clutching palms
laughing into the centre of
the storm as they spin
faster and faster
invoking the serpent of Shakti to rise.

Connected into the heartbeat of Gaia and her cleansing ritual
we bless each other with a reverent touch
to the heart, to the womb and to the temples.

Each sister smiles with a remembrance of generational union.

Breathing in the depths of a long journey
back into the blood
of our sisterhood.

Each and every experience here,
profound
unique
and purposeful.

The blessing is already given
cultivated and discovered within…
The altar continued to hold
a crystalline vision of deep passion and power where
all of creation is birthed

The citrine crystals warmly shine
joining in the dance, long into the night.

Oils and floral perfumes pour from vials
onto the spine of a disheartened Goddess,

hurt by the masks of the fallen
they hold space for her receiving
of loving attention:
Her birthright.

Allowing the warm oils to trickle down her spine
she listens to the song of the rain joining in
to bless and cleanse her of any unworthy fears.

Completely releasing into this platonic intimacy
she is covered in the blessing of acceptance and liberation.

She falls into a bed of roses that gently kiss
her breasts,
her cheeks
her belly
and womb.

"It's like I never left," she softly smiles.
And the circle replies,

"None of us ever left,
we only forgot."

GODDESS BLESSING RITUAL GUIDANCE

Ritual Ingredients:

>   Candles
>   Sisterhood
>   Chanting music
>   Essential oils
>   Rose water
>   Rose petals

Gather with sisters to enjoy this powerful ritual of acceptance and celebration of the Goddess. It is a very powerful practice of communication about the way you feel about the Goddess when you bless one of your sisters and celebrate her fully in reverence to the moment.

Have rose water ready to be passed around in a large bowl with some essential oils ready as well of your choice. First, you will want to open your space with a mantra that allows all of the sisters to feel comfortable to open up and connect with each other. Sit in a circle and each repeat this mantra by turning to each other on the left as the mantra goes around the circle:

'I release my ego now and listen with an open heart. In perfect trust, In perfect love, we are all one in this sacred space.' Seal the spell by having each Goddess bless the sister to their left (after saying the mantra) and placing essential oils into the rose water. Have her bless the sister to her left by having her cleanse her sisters hands with the rose water and by placing one drop of the water upon her third eye, temples, throat and heart chakra.

Once everyone has said the mantra and blessed each other with the water, the circle has been sealed with the protection of sacred light. You can begin to chant or sing a mantra by holding hands and spinning in a circle as the chant becomes louder and stronger. The chant can be any song you wish to use, it might be a Sanskrit mantra or a song that resonates deeply with you.

Once the chant has ended, stand strong with your sisters in silence and reverence with your eyes closed. Breathe and take in one Cosmic OM. Then, choose one sister to bless in the centre of the circle. Create a nest for her to lay in as you all bless and worship her body with the water and oils. Gently surround her with rose petals and let her take in the powerful blessing of reverence as you all gently caress her skin.

LIONESS BOUNDARIES RITUAL

I open my eyes
into the wild riviera.
A starborn force
rolling in the trees.

Naked to the jungle
I fear nothing beneath my feet
as I hunt to kill.

The lions rush to aid me in my will to feast
but I know the final glory will be in flowing lightly
with the changing winds.

Silence.

My fastened gaze upon the horizon.
I watch my prey oblivious to my sight.

One silent drop of a far off leaf
and I pounce into the darkness to revel in the flesh
of what will quench
my undying thirst to strike.

AND STILL
I do not feast on my victory…

I stand readily, seeking to protect
this sacred circle of life I call home.

And so I welcome you.

In reverence to this heart …
as a guest…

May you enter.

BOUNDARIES RITUAL

Ritual Ingredients:

Spell Jar:

>Red candle to signify desire
>Small glass vial or jar
>Resin of Copal
>Optional: Osha Root
>Tiny crystals of Obsidian or Blood Stone
>Cork-top to seal vial

In this ritual, we will be calling in the spirit-essence of the lion and the bear by creating a spell jar for you to bring with you wherever you go.

First, set up a sacred space that is protected from other energies with soothing music that resonates with you. Close your eyes and take a deep breath in and out to ground into the moment. Honour the space and call in Goddess Kali to support you in cutting any cords to entities that are not serving you. Also ask her to guide you towards a higher realm of self-respect so that you can set powerful boundaries and communicate them from a place of love. Open your eyes and light your red candle to begin the ritual.

As you chant the mantra Wahe Guru by Shiuli Subaya (I am darkness to light) begin to place your resin of Copal into the jar with the intention of sending the blood of the Protium tree to the Goddess. Copal is offered to the Goddess to honour the enormous sacred gift of life given to us by all the tree people of our planet. Copal is the blood that is offered back to the Earth and the Gods when the tree is worshiped and respected. When the tree is loved, respected and happy, the Copal is offered more freely. Place this into the vial with respect to our tree people of the Earth.

Place your choosing of obsidian crystals into the vile with the intention of protection from heavy or taxing energy. People that will not serve your highest good will not be attracted to you anymore and will fall away from your auric-field. If you have chosen the blood-stone, place this crystal into your jar with the intention of increased intuition. This will allow you to feel into your gut when people cross your boundaries. You will be able to trust your intuition and give them the consequences they need to respect your boundaries and remember that people like and admire respectful relationships; these relationships are worth more.

Optional: Place your Osha Root into your spell jar with the intention of calling in the spirit of the bear. The bear spirit represents grounding forces and strength. This will give you the courage to stand up against adversity and situations not in alignment with your higher-self. Remember, kindness is not weakness, but standards, morals and values can be communicated with a sense of calm, steady strength.

Once the chanting mantra has ended, you can smudge your spell jar in Palo Santo to amplify its intentions. Then take your red candle and pour the melted wax around the cork lid to seal the spell with care.

Let the jar cool and integrate the intention by placing it somewhere special with crystals and amplified energy overnight. Take this special gift from The Goddess with you wherever you go to stay true to yourself.

Many blessings.

MOON CYCLE RITUAL

I felt for the first time the waves of her Reign
rushing through my womb.

She gave me the scent of the nectar
And approached me with reverence.

And when I tasted the sweet Goddess,
She anointed me with grace.
I felt the blessing rush into the doors of my heart
— severing every resentment and gave me back my life.

The crown now rests gently upon my head
I no longer sit at the foot of her Palace
but recognize her entire Queendom
within my velvet flowing river.

FULL MOON CYCLE RITUAL GUIDANCE

Ritual Ingredients:

>   White candle to represent the inner-child
>   Red candle to represent the Goddess
>   Optional: Vial to place womb-blood
>   Optional: Cup of red wine
>   Red velvet cupcake
>   Rose petals and rose water
>   Ylang Ylang or Lavender essential oils

This ritual can be used for a woman who has 1. Just received her first ever moon cycle, 2. For a Goddess that is coming into her crone cycle of syncing her menstruation to the full moon 3. For a woman who is or has received her menopausal glow.

Set your space with love, either alone in your *Goddess Nest* or with sisters in a circle. Light the white candle and read the 'My Inner Child' poem on page 64 as a symbol of reverence to the journey of your past. Then light the red candle and place the vial of womb-blood or cup of red wine in-between the two candles in reverence to Mother Nature.

Recite the mantra ' Grandmother Moon' on page 60 as a sign of reverence to the gifts we receive through our cycles and maturing into our golden years of wisdom. If you're using a vial of your womb-blood, mix some of the rose water with the blood and dip your finger into the vile to anoint yourself upon your third-eye and anywhere else upon your body you're drawn to. The rose womb-blood will honour this moment of passage Grandmother Moon has gifted you with.

If you are using a cup of red wine, take a sip of the wine and feel it travel down your throat through your heart chakra and into your solar plexus. Then take the rest of the wine, place an intention of gratitude for your life into the wine (or vial of blood) and go outside where you can mix it with the soil and offer it back into the Earth with reverence for the knowledge she offers us.

After this beautiful right of passage, take some time to celebrate this new cycle, crone cycle or menopausal status by adorning your body with the blessing of rose water, rose petals and covering your feet and pelvis with Ylang-Ylang oil or Lavender oil with care.

If you're wanting to be even more celebratory with this ritual, enjoy some red velvet cake to consummate the ritual with sensual joy and love for the Goddess and her wisdom.

Side Note: ***Remember that the Crone Cycle (syncing your cycle to the full moon) is a very special time in a woman's life as it signifies when a woman is being called to share her treasures with the Earth and its creatures. The moon is asking you to be in service to the world around you because you have many gifts and gems of wisdom to offer.

The Goddess of Creation is synched to the full moon and births gifts that will help awaken and elevate the world around her. Never forget to stay in the art of receiving by giving yourself the love you deserve at all times so you're working from a full cup.***

To close the ritual of reverence to Grandmother Moon's magic, blow out the white candle and allow the red candle to burn into the night as long as you would like. Then read the poem 'Mystic Relations' on page 19.

Many blessings.

THE GODDESS NEST RITUAL

Wombyn in the garden of roses.
unowned by anyone
she is only in service to the cosmos
guiding her abundant awakening.

Resting in the garden of faith
she lays her head gently on a blanket of stars
she sips from a honey jar of sweet nectar
nourishing her veins of purity.

Roses ripely open towards her as she goes in and in.
Serving herself potent deep connection,
she is offered gifts from Mother Gaia
she so rightfully adorns her body in.

Feet dipped in cold sunlit water
she ingratiates her legs in the dance of rose-drops
flowing down cleansing life-blood back into the Earth
sealing this sacred ritual.

She listens to the sound-healing of the water blessing
and invokes a reiki-dance with each drop
grateful for the blessing of intention.

The glow of candles
call in her ancestors.

Clouds moving steadily by…

"I recognize you," She says.

The leaves falling in slow motion around her
and she remembers…

"The sky was there for me—
and the ground was vast.
so so endless… into your Labyrinth."

And she recognizes the spirit of the Rose calling to her.
It showed itself to her when all forms of language came to a halt.
And without the human touch to keep them from each other,
They began to blend into one another.

Not friends, not lovers….
Unity.

She welcomed the rose to be rooted deep into her womb and said,

"Release your divine kiss here," whispering,
"It will land in my heart."

And the golden light of the rose set a tantric fire
within her that resounded for centuries
breaking down patterns of harm…

Only to worship herself once again.

RITUAL GUIDANCE

Ritual Ingredients:

>Blanket
>Pillows (as many as you'd like)
>Candles
>Crystals of your choice
>Flowers of your choice
>Rose water
>Optional: Cacao elixir or tea
>Fruit to eat of your choice
>Music
>Something cozy to wear or adorn your body in a special fabric that makes you feel protected
>Sage of your choice
>Incense
>Crushed Egg Shells, Selenite or Himalayan Salt

Welcome to your Goddess Nest creation ritual, Goddess! Here we will create a space that makes you feel completely loved, supported and pampered. This space can take many forms, in fact, it can be different every single time and that's the fun of creating ritual! This space can even take form in the bath if you wish at times.

To begin, choose a space within your home or outside that has some privacy so you can feel completely held within your own energy. Take some time to feel into your body before you begin the creation process and write down what your intention is for wanting to sit in your *Goddess Nest* today. This intention will inform your creation process along the way so take some time to check-in without judgment and focus on your intuition.

First choose a cozy blanket that will be soft and comfortable to lay on as well as some pillows to hold the nest in softness. If you have selenite crystals you can place them around the nest to support the amplification of energetic healing. If you do not have selenite, you can surround the nest with either Himalayan pink salt to clear the energy around you or use crushed egg shells (which have a high frequency) for protection of the space from lower vibration entities.

Then place the flowers, fruits and other crystals you have intentionally chosen to have with you today in your *Goddess Nest*. Once you've placed these items, you have the option to sprinkle rose petals upon the nest and smudge the area to clear the space.

I love to light a candle and some incense to activate the energy once I am settled in the nest. Here I read the poem on page 93 for this ritual and begin by playing a mantra to chant to. The chant can be in Sanskrit or in English. A beautiful mantra to sing too is, 'I am perfect as I am,' by Beautiful Chorus and then relax into the Hymn 'Faith's Hymn' by Beautiful Chorus.

Here you can relax into the knowing that your nest is protected, high-vibration and is here to catch you with whatever emotion comes up here. Allow your feelings to rise up and embrace them through the art of meditation, painting, reading, ritual, singing, resting, writing, blessing yourself with rose water and oils or just staring up at the sky. The choice is yours, sweet Goddess. This is your time to rest and recalibrate in the royal nest of high-frequency worship for the Goddess within.

Sat Nam.

GODDESS MANIFESTATION RITUAL

I close my eyes and I am there.
Already in the moment of my finest hour.

I see myself with
glowing eyes and a smile
that glows like stars in the dark.

This Goddess has all she
could ever want in life.
Her purpose shines from her
heart as she serves the world
with the magic God granted.

She steps into her truth with honour
and weeps with those who need her.

She is surrounded by love that is
as fine as her own heart reflection.

Dancing into the night she
floats with glee and gratitude
to live another day.

She rejoices in
her own personal heaven she called-in
when she set down who she
thought she should be
and claimed all that she
actually is.

Without the need to appease anyone
she knows who she is and
what she wants out of her days.

The people and places in her life
are placed like a painting she
works on daily.

And so I create a work of art
that is in alignment with her, my higher-self

and I honour
this gift everyday by walking
in the light of my creator.

I paint with passion
and feel with deep intention.

I am everything and everything is me.
And the world smiles in celebration of my arrival.

GODDESS MANIFESTATION RITUAL

The most potent way to cast this ritual is to first create a Goddess Nest Ritual, found on page 94.

If you would just like to have a quick manifestation ritual, just simply find a space that is quiet and comfortable.

Ritual Ingredients:

>Cozy blanket
>Candle
>Journal and pen
>Meditation cushion
>Tea of your choice
>Protection shawl
>Optional: Roses
>Optional: Magnolia essential oil

This ritual is so much more effective when done everyday for 10 days or more. Find a comfortable space either in your nest or somewhere you feel happy. Sit upon your meditation cushion and place your protection shawl around your shoulders. This shawl does not have to be any specific type of shawl, just one that makes you feel protected and serene.

Place your roses close by as a sign of abundance and respect for your higher-self. Let's take a moment to light the candle and activate the ritual with closed eyes, a tall spine and a soft belly. Take your awareness into your belly and feel the energy pulsing here. What does it feel like? Again, without judging this feeling... let's assign a colour and a shape to it. Notice where it is living within your body and then breathe for three full counts into this space... hold the breath here for two counts.

Breathe out for four full breaths and continue this cycle of breath for five minutes. Come back to your natural breath and invite a waterfall of white golden light to cloak your body here. Allow the light of the Universe to receive, cleanse and heal you as you breathe into the space of tension.

Breathing steadily and consciously with your eyes closed, try to bring your awareness to your third eye and breathe in a calming blue light through the centre of your forehead… then exhale to expand this light down through your heart and belly. Continue this cycle of light-work for seven conscious cycles of breath.

Then let go of your breath and just sit in the calm, steady stillness of your natural beauty. Listen to the silence or to the sounds around you… now take your awareness inwards and as you softly breathe, envision yourself somewhere that makes you feel joyful. Take a moment to witness what you're wearing in this vision and where you are. Where are you standing and how does it feel? What do you see?

You envision yourself living in your truth and smiling as you go about your day. You have an inner-knowing and confidence about you. A radiance that shines from within… notice what you are doing and where you are going? Who is in your life? As you stay with the vision, notice the energy you feel when you see yourself living your most authentic life. Breathe into this energy in your belly and expand this energy throughout your entire body. Envision yourself all it up with the Universal light like a bright ball of high-vibration energy.

Notice in your visions now what creations you are offering to others around you. Notice the gratitude from the world in recognition of you walking in your truth and in your passion. Breathe in all the love from your life, events, people and places around you. Feel this gratitude to live within the heart and to walk in your most authentic-self. Notice your higher-self smiling and expressing her truth with humility and confidence.

She walks with joy into her future and lives presently with clarity and love.

Breathe in all of this abundance and let it turn into a waterfall of light once again—-taking over your entire body. Let it fill you with love, peace and gratitude as you take in the frequency of passion and become fully present with your higher-self journey.

After 10-20 minutes of feeling the frequency of this higher-self Universe that awaits you… take time to let this energy be integrated into your cells to calibrate. In time, open your eyes and softly take a look around you at all the blessings that currently surround you. Pick up your journal and pen and write down what you saw in your visions, where you were and what you were doing. Write down the people you saw and how they responded to your energy in the vision.

Once you are done writing your vision down, take some time to read it out load into the ethers. Then close the ritual of your vision by blowing out the candle and reciting the mantra: 'And so it is.'

Now that you have embodied this frequency, keep building it within you for nine more days to cultivate more of a magnetic vibration. What is so interesting scientifically about this practice is that the mind does not know the difference between a vision and reality or past, present and future. This means that the mind believes your vision is already happening to you presently and so it sends hormones and chemicals to the body that align your energetic-state with this vision; ultimately attracting to you what you feel inside.

This is the true key to manifestation; Envision it, feel it, embody the energetic state and then subsequently you will attract what you're feeling so it can become a reality for you. Accept this blessing as a natural state of your being, instead of believing it is outside of you.

Remember, if it exists in your mind and on the Astral Plane (where anything we can envision in co-creation with the Universe already exists and is possible) it can be birthed into this realm as well.
Believe. BE. Receive.

Close this powerful ritual by placing the writing of your vision in a manifestation box or jar, while singing the chant: 'I am Surrounded by Love' by Beautiful Chorus, sipping your tea to cleanse and covering yourself with magnolia oil to call in abundance and self-love.

Many blessings to your path forward!

WHITE BUFFALO SAGING RITUAL

I watch you dance around me, Gaia.

Smoke like magic
you incase the air
with a cleansing
vibration of peace.

Ultimate restoration for my sanity
you create a dream in this
realm like a bridge-point
between Heaven and Earth.

White Buffalo of creation,
I dance with you into thin air
past the veil into another dimension.

Thank you for clearing a pathway
for this deep conversation
with my heart.

White Buffalo of healing
become a circle of protection
for the most vulnerable words
of honesty and truth.

Let your smoke dance
in a circle around me
washing away this heaviness
I have cradled for so long.

Sage around the soles of my feet
and bring me a song of a steady drum
reminding me of this
pranic-force within
and the infinite love you
have to offer.

Forever & ever I bow to you…

and she answers,

"Dear child, let me sit with you."

SAGING RITUAL GUIDANCE

Ritual Ingredients:

    White Buffalo Sage

This ritual is to cleanse your energetic-field, your space and your journey forward. Before you light the sage, greet it with kindness and ask the Divine Mother for cleansing and recalibration of heavy energy back into its natural state of divine love.

As you light the sage, try not to place it directly into the flame as to show the Mother gratitude and respect. Just gently graze the sage with the tip of the flame so as to not create a fire. Then sway the sage back and forth to gently put the flame out and allow the smoke to dance. (Try not to blow on the sage or the flame… this is seen as disrespectful to the medicine.) Let the sage dance on its own and approach you with ease and of its own resolve.

As the smoke grazes your body, you can relax and take it in or chant a prayer into the smoke as it eases and clears the space around you. Feel the spirit of the Mother approaching you and anointing you with her divinity to be of support and protection for you to speak to her with honesty and vulnerable truth.

Sit in her enveloping hug of wavering smoke and feel a softness begin to emerge from within. Smell the grounding force of her elemental flow and bring your awareness to your sit bones sitting steady upon her Earth as she holds you here.

If you feel called… ask her a question or feel free to call on your ancestors here to speak to you with love and guidance. Press the sage into an Abalone Shell or a smudging bowl to put it out completely.

Lastly, I like to bow to the smudge with gratitude for this space to sit with the Mother and listen to her songs, feel her grace, dance with her and call in the spirits of the present.

SELF LOVE OIL RITUAL

I wrap my beloved body in these blanketing oils.
Every flower essence kissing my skin,
Cloaking me in the jewels of Gaia.

Touching and blessing every inch
of this sweet vessel that allows me to feel.
This embrace reminds me how much
I've cried for the divine Goddess in my bones.

Tears running down my cheeks as I surrender to all that I am.
A river of blessings sweeps through my hair.
Silky on my fingertips.
Shining just for me.
Massaging. Feeling.

Elbows
Collarbones
Heart Centre
Cheeks
Lips
Hands…
Glorious Hands.

I gaze at this blessed face in the mirror.
This very face that has live through
lives, essences, darkness, freedom & loss.

Finally free to truly see …
my tears begin to fall.
And I whisper into the gaze of the beloved Goddess within —

"I love you into all the nights of
the moon and into the light of acceptance, sweet one.

You. Are. Beautiful."

SELF LOVE OIL RITUAL GUIDANCE

Ritual Ingredients:

Option of:
    Apricot oil
    Coconut oil
    Almond oil
    or Jojoba oil
    Few drop of lavender oil

After a long relaxing bath, simply dry yourself off and take a few nourishing tablespoons of the oil of your choice. In this Ayurvedic practice, you can take time to honour each part of your body as you massage the oil into your feet, legs, belly and all your many other beautiful areas of this blessed vessel.

With this ritual, it's important to take extra time to truly feel and honour your body. This is the vessel that works and honours you every single second of the day. You may want to listen to some sound-healing music or hum to your body as you ingratiate yourself with the nectar of Gaia (the oil of your choice).

Cover yourself in a beautiful veil of oil and even run it through your hair for a softening treatment for luscious hair. You can leave the oil in overnight or wash it out in the shower after. You can also let the oil seep into your skin and cover your body in soft lingerie to sleep.

Once you have covered your body in oil… feel free to take this self-love ritual one step further for deep subconscious healing and look into the mirror. Clasp your cheeks with your palms in reverence to your beauty. Gaze deep into your eyes and say the following passage with genuine self-love (which is very difficult at first):

"I love you.
I want you to know you are absolutely beautiful,
I love you Goddess,
I honour all that you are,
I love you so much,
You. Are. Divine.
I love you.
Thank you for being here for me.
I am so proud of you."

Engage in this ritual everyday for 30 days and it is said in the Ayurvedic tradition that you will truly learn to love your body. This ritual is a form of a Goddess blessing and a sign to the Universe that you are grateful for your body as well as for the essence of your higher-self.

With this attention you're giving your Goddess essence she will soon feel welcomed into your consciousness and will come alive in your day-to-day life to play & guide you towards a life that is full of love and grace.

THE ALTAR-SPACE

I place my emotions onto
the throne of creation and the bridge-point that
cradles my heart with Heaven.

The angels view my potent
gratitude that shines off the glistening
fruit of life that rest here for them to take.

The offering is a karmic release
that is gifted into the wild wisdom
of my teacher.

The Goddess.

Her playful knowledge gives
lessons through the art of feeling.

Wombyn can sink deep into
their awakenings with pain and powerful gifts.

She knows the power
these gifts offer
and so she lays with
her heart wide open
as she portrays an almighty truth.

She knows without the altar her
connection is not lost
however it is sealed with a kiss
upon the placement of each symbol.

Her angels watch as she
co-creates a work of art
through the Goddess in nature.

Placing each talisman
with a soft and intuitive touch
she whispers…

'Thank you, forgive me, I'm sorry, I love you.'

THE ALTAR-SPACE RITUAL

A great way to open a ceremony is an altar-placing and blessing.

Ritual Ingredients:

    1. Location: An altar-space can be:
On the floor with a blanket
Out in nature in a sacred place
On a table or corner of a room.

    2. Talismans: Talismans are items that contain a high-frequency such as;
Crystals
Flowers
Incense
Fruit
Money
Photos of Ancestors or loved ones
Resin
Sage
Plant medicine
Anything that has sentimental value.

The Benefits of An Altar:

Altars are created by people of many different religions and traditions. These sacred places of reverence can be found in temples, churches, natural places, and historical sites. People who love the feeling of these sacred spaces also create them in their homes and use this ritual as a way to support their spiritual connection to Source.

Altars act as a bridge-point where the physical realm merges with ethereal realms and where we can readily meet with Source energy, the gods, our higher-selves, angels, guides, and our ancestors. By setting up an altar, you are establishing sacred space – a safe, comfortable place to focus on your spiritual growth and the growth of others to amplify energetic space within this realm.

How to Set Up An Altar:

Setting up an altar-space is a beautiful and creative art-form to connect to your higher-self and this case, The Goddess within.

First, decide where you'd like to create your altar-space. It can be a permanent place where you will always have ceremony or a present space for a one-time ritual. If you'd like to set one up in your home, a beautiful desk, hallway table, end table or even a meditation table is a beautiful way to honour your connection to Source. Here you can set up candles and crystals that resonate with your heart and the energy you want to call into your life. You can also place a box or a bowl where you write notes of prayer either to release or call-in energy, or to give gratitude.

I personally use my permanent altar-space in my home for full moon rituals where I can connect to the energy of the moment and listen for messages from The Goddess.

Another question asked regularly is which direction the altar should face – north, south, east, or west?

The direction of your altar really depends on your belief-system or spiritual intention. In Wiccan traditions, altars face north in the direction of the element of Earth. In some eastern traditions, altars face east towards the rising sun. You can also change the direction each day depending on the direction of the winds or your gratitude to the seven spiritual directions. Ultimately an altar set-up is intuitive and so if a direction is calling you, you may want to listen to that message and honour it.

Talismans or items of the highest vibration are used in relation to nature and the elements. Each tool is thought to represent each of the five elements found in nature.

A cauldron or symbol of plant medicine can represent Earth. Incense or sage represents air, candles represent the fire element, and shells or a jar of moon water can represent the water for emotional aspects of your ceremony.

Other sacred items for your altar may include crystals, plants, statues, tarot cards, flowers, books and the list goes on. Incense is also used as an offering to deities and ancestors to carry messages up to the Heavens.

Sitting with your altar-space and meditating after the creation and intention portion is necessary as a sign of reverence to the beloved Universal pool of knowledge available to you once your altar has been created. Think of your altar-space as a portal into the unknown etheric realms of mystery and conscious elevation.

Your intention is the most valuable ingredient when working with an altar-space. Why are you setting up or sitting with an altar-space? How do you feel? What are wanting to ask The Goddess? Are you hurting or are you feeling grateful? Are you in need of guidance or are you calling in your higher-self to be fully embodied? Is there a specific Goddess or God you would like to connect with in your life? This is a sacred gateway to ask these energies to come into your life and to show themselves to you in ways you can understand.

The intentions can be endless, but the more specific you are with this practice, the more powerful your connection will be with your altar-space. I hope this ritual serves you and that you find some joyful moments in this playful and sincere act of connection with the Goddess. The portal of the altar creation has been one of the most powerful moments of reflection in my life and in the lives of so many for centuries.

BREAKING THE RITUAL OF TRAUMA
(AN INTERLUDE)

I choose to not
engage in this Ritual of Trauma.

I will not walk
in the opposite direction of my ultimate
goal: inner peace.

The goal of my life is not to control
the outcome of other people
or experiences, but to
call-in peace.

Every time I engage in my need to control
I know I am engaging in my own personal
Ritual of Trauma.

I choose to let go of what I cannot control
and let love lead the way.

CACAO GODDESS

Sweet paste of chocolate feminine glory
opening my heart into bliss.

This first taste dances on my tongue
ingratiating my being with divinity and love.

I feel no calculation or agendas here.
They all fall away
to be recalibrated back into eminence.

Her comforting scent fills the room with
magic welcomed by the hearts of so many.

I feel at home in her presence as she
seeps deep into my heart chakra
to remind me of how marvellous we all are.

She was birthed in a cocoon from a tree
in a place that is warm and wild.

Yet, I feel so connected to her and the soil
of which she came.

I've waited for her to calm my heart
and take me back to an essence
I emanated long ago when I was a child.

I dance and celebrate and move her
veil of worship through my entire being
as she plays through me like an instrument.
She offers to me what I need most.

I relax into the gaze of others
and dance with their energy so joyful and true.

We are love upon love
and we dance into the night
feeling the joyful beat,
liberated in the celebration of being.

It is the Cacao that brought us here
to connect to the dance of life
and to play in the sweetness
of our very own existence.

Here in the heart of cacao
we witness each other
in the bliss-point of salvation.

THE CACAO GODDESS RITUAL

(AN OFFERING OF TRANSFORMATION FOR THE HEART)

A cacao ceremony is an opportunity to connect to yourself and open your heart. Because of cacao's ability to increase your connection to your inner and higher-self and your heart chakra, it aids in spiritual transformational shifts.

A cacao ceremony is a very safe and intimate space and the people that attend in the dance with you are always surprised at how they are able to open up to others, especially when they realize that we are all a mirror for each other. One of the main active ingredients that we experience with cacao is Theo-broma, which translates as God-Food, and heightens the release of dopamine, the 'pleasure' hormone. This, alongside phenethylamine, which helps relieve stress and depression and is released in the body during emotional euphoria, creates a heightened sensation of empathy and relaxation. Everything feels heightened within the physical and emotional body, including your awareness to your deepest sense of self and to your heart.

The resonating after-effects of a cacao ceremony is increased love and empathy for yourself and the world around you. This practice heightens your frequency and allows you to become a more conscious and enlightened being of light. You can sit with cacao in meditation, simply by making a cacao elixir. Cacao paste is a great ingredient because it includes all the natural fats of the cacao bean. which allows the nutrients to be accepted into the body with ease. Once the cacao has melted in boiling water, you can add cinnamon, maca powder, reishi mushroom, honey (once in cup) and even a little bit of cayenne pepper to taste if you'd like a little more heat. Welcome the blessing of cacao into your body like a warm hug from Gaia. More cacao recipes can be found online at keithscacao.com.

THE FOURTH PRECEPT
(HOLDING SPACE RITUAL)

We sit here together and prepare
to open and receive
the pain you so courageously share.

Without the need to fix you
I listen with honour.

Here we are safe
to share without judgement
and to speak into a silent ritual of healing.

I promise to be the sounding-board
that will allow you to heal yourself.

I hold space to receive you fully
and stay comfortable in the moments
of silence that provide time to integrate
and open with words that may have
never been said.

This is your time.
Not mine.
I am in service to you
and I promise to listen
without condition or perception.

My ears are open
and I release my ego now.

I listen with an open heart
and let these words that are shared
never leave my mouth
once we walk away.

In perfect trust,
In perfect love,
We are one presence.

HOLDING SPACE RITUAL

A great way to open a ceremony is an altar placing and blessing.

Ritual Ingredients:

> Sage
> A candle
> Tissues
> Optional: Crushed egg shells
> Optional: Tea

The fourth precept is a powerful ceremony that allows the person you care about to fully and completely their emotional heart pain without being fixed or judged.

This is a Buddhist practice that allows for healing and preparation for conscious elevation to let go and prepare for connection with the world. The fourth precept has 3 rules when holding space for someone:

1. Open space and make the other person feel safe
2. Do not hug the person if they need to cry as this closes them off from expressing emotions and subconsciously communicates to them that you want them to stop crying.
3. Do not show any facial expressions so as to not make them think you are accepting or denying their feelings.
4. Do not speak, nod, or try to fix their problems but simply hold space and silence for them like a protection warrior for them fully express feelings and know that the floor is there's and that your are simply receiving them in your heart.

This practice may take a long time so set aside enough time for some difficult emotions to be processed. It is very hard to practice rule number 2, because it's hard to not comfort someone when they are feeling down or crying because that is our natural response to pain. But it is a very powerful practice to simply just let someone BE in the moment of their processing while having a sounding board to witness them fully without judgement. This practice takes time and experience. This is the power of listening and receiving without engaging. You'll begin to see the person you love open up and even begin to heal themselves in the presence of your undivided attention. Hold space in the silence, which at times may be uncomfortable. Be the warrior that holds this silence no matter what for them. This is where some of the most important processing can happen for them and the release of pain begin. Have tissues near by for them.

You can light the candle to begin the session and sage the space to clear residual energy that may influence the conversation. The most important part of this ritual is allow the other person to feel completely safe and comfortable so you may want to create a *Goddess Nest* for them or simply make them some tea. You can also crush some egg shells to seal the circle of trust around you both by sprinkling the shells around the circle.

To close the session when they have said with their own words to you that they are done, you can tell them you honour them for showing up and sharing their truth. Bow to them and tell them you see them in all their glory and honesty.

This is the power of holding space for someone.

TINGLES: A CALMING RITUAL

She runs her fingertips gently
down my skin slowly bringing me
back into the moment.

Tracing down my spine
all the way to my sacrum
and gently tapping across my
shoulders…

I begin to feel grounded
in this body as I
sink free into every sensation.

The platonic intimacy from
Goddess to Goddess
is like a true blessing from an angel.

I am grateful for this body to feel
sweet tingles of serenity
and the comfort of friendship.

Brushing my long hair
down my back
my scalp accepts this
softness like a waterfall of light
healing and recalibrating
my auric field.

She whispers into my ears
the angelic sounds
of honour, presence
and compassionate grace.

This softness expands
through my palms and feet
as my lips begin to part and my
jaw falls open.

> All the tiny muscles around
> my eyes relax as my forehead
> becomes serene and smooth.
>
> I feel the connection to bliss.
>
> "You're beautiful," she says…
>
> and she leaves me to bask in this
> nest of tingly feathered energy.
>
> A nesting devotion to softness
> in my own floating body…
> unwilling to open my eyes.

TINGLES RITUAL GUIDANCE

Ritual Ingredients:

> A feather
> Water and essential oils of your choice in a spray bottle
> Soft hair brush

The tingled ritual requires you to sit with a sister or someone you feel truly safe with and loved. This is a platonic intimate ritual between friends to admire and bless the body and existence of someone. First choose is you will be receiving the blessing or if you will be giving it.

The sister who is receiving will sit in front and the sister who is giving the blessing will sit behind, either in chairs or on the floor. Have the Goodess who is receiving either remove her shirt of have her back somewhat available to touch. First have the Goddess who is receiving close her eyes and takes a deep breath as you begin to run the feather down her spine. Have her surrender to the touch by reminding her it is safe to relax by placing your hands on her shoulders and pressing down gently to ground her into her body. You can also run your hands through her hair and very lightly pull her hair from the root to have her senses ground into your touch. Then run your fingertips from her head down over her shoulders slowly as you bless her. Only continue if she is relaxed and ready to engage in the act of receiving. Continue with spraying around her body with the water and essential oils by clearing her aura with this scent.

You can continue the ritual by slowly brushing her hair down her back lightly to give her tingles. if her hair is knotted, grab her in a pony tail and brush the ends of her hair first and then work your way up to the scalp. Continue to brush lightly until her hair is silky smooth.

Finish with some back tracing with the feather up the spine and onto her front of her chest and shoulders. You can even use the feather on her face with her eyes closed if she is comfortable with this. Remember to move slowly and with intention by blessing her skin and her auric field. Remember this practice is powerful as it sets her back into her body and it also shows you reverence for the vessel of the Goddess and the recognition of her essence within you like a reflection of what you to desire to receive. The more love you place into this ritual, the more you will receive.

Enjoy and breathe in the touch with every tingle. Remember this is a platonic intimate touching ritual so if you choose to conduct this ritual with a lover, try to keep it platonic so you can truly receive the blessing without the goal of anything else.

THE MESSAGES SHE WOULD HAVE ME READ
(FREE WRITING RITUAL)

Sweet silence
permeating deep into
my oceanic eye …

The colours float like
systematic closure
that displays the merging of
shades within my heart.

The greys that once seemed to
differentiate now blend together in a sweet
silhouette of unity.

I open up as a channel
and listen to the words
of her presence
as they prance onto
the page before me.

It's a vortex of infinite wisdom
when she pours out to me.

All has passed and it's just
us here as we dance
into symphonic chorus
of careless freedom.

I see with my own eyes
the messages she would have me read.

And in these words
she honours every pathway
I've travelled.

Now is the time…
I am ready to listen.
I am ready to receive her.

No bittersweet love known.

She cannot be lost.

I cry into her soft embrace and sing
lullabies with the moon
as she cradles and holds me here
on a steady stone …

I witness her unwavering hold.

To be in her sweet embrace,
she is the only place I truly feel grace.

Filling up pages without condition,
she bares her entire soul with mine…

She is the reality, here:
Where there is nothing unseen.

And I see with my own eyes
the messages she would have me read.

FREE WRITING RITUAL

Ritual Ingredients:

> Journal
> Pen
> Meditation space and cushion
> Optional supporting tools include: Crystals, sage and a white candle to represent transcendence/openness.

To begin this ritual you will want to meditate for a minimum of 10 minutes before-hand. You may choose a guided meditation, which you can find on my YouTube Channel: Ananda Cait ASMR or through another audio tool available on your phone or online. Once the mind is quiet, The Goddess can speak to us from the heart-space. You will want to work on quieting your mind and if your mind is very loud and busy, begin by engaging in something active like yoga, pranayama or another form of exercise to release stagnant energy. Once you have worked this stagnant energy out of your system, you will be ready to begin the meditation.

1. Light the white candle and then close your eyes to take three deep breaths in and out. Fully inflating the lungs and then fully contracting the lungs to release all the old air out.
2. Envelope in a calming meditation for 10 - 20 minutes. Allow this meditation to be a form of conscious rest you can embrace as there are many different types of meditations.
3. Once you have finished your meditation, set a timer for 10 minutes and stay silent as you pick up your pen and place it to paper.
4. Write for 10 full minutes without thinking about what you're going to write. Even if the words and phrasing do not make sense, keep writing no matter what. Try not to stop for 10 minutes and let whatever comes out on the page just flow!
5. Now you can read the writing back to yourself and circle words and phrases that resonate with you. You may find that the Universe has written you a message of deep resonance. Keep the writing in a sacred place as it may resonate further with you in the future.
6. To close this ritual, blow out the candle and repeat the mantra, 'I am free where I am, and I am open to receiving the messages of the cosmos. I thank you for this life.'

FULL MOON RITUALS

I collect these petals as a sign of love
and gratitude for our Divine Mother.

The gems of the season
are gifted to me with a sense of reverence.
I place them on the altar
to ignite this gratitude within my heart.

Let me always be this grateful for Mother
and let me see her gifts holding me here with awareness of the constant
change I see within her.

The ground lets go as I weep with joy to
experience a new day,
a new season,
a new night with her.

She sparks a new star within my eyes of infinite belonging.
I see her glory
over and over again.
Gaia's gifts lay gently upon her altar
as I let her distinctly write intentions through me.

How may I birth your
presence on this full moon?

How may I elevate within
the wisdom of the Divine Grandmother?

Her light shines upon me
as I soak her gems lightly in moon-water.

With every intention to embrace and surrender to her
I release her wild-blood back into this light-reflected ocean:
Her messenger into the sky.

SEASONAL FULL MOON RITUAL GUIDANCE

.I Ingredients:

<u>For winter season</u>:
Pinecones/leaves/twigs/sand/rocks

<u>For spring season:</u>
In-season floral petals

<u>For summer season:</u>
In-season floral petals
In-season fruit/vegetables

<u>For autumn season:</u>
Fallen leaves/in-season flowers/in-season fruit or vegetables

<u>For all full moon rituals:</u>
Journal
Sage
Plant medicine of your choice (Cacao, Hapé, Ganja or Water to drink)
Candle of your choice
Bowl or cup of water

1. Light the candle and repeat the following mantra three times:
- 'Thank you Grandmother Moon for shining your light upon me and birthing something new once again. I am an open channel for your energy to shine through, please show me what I need to know from your wisdom and allow me to receive your messages in a way I can fully comprehend along this next lunar cycle. Show me what needs to be birthed through me. In precious love, In precious trust. Amen.'

2. Light your sage with reverence to Mother Earth and clear the space to ground and quiet the mind. Let it dance through the air as you chant the mantra: "Earth my body, Water my blood, Air my breath and Fire my spirit."

3. Take some time to write down what is coming up for you this particular night and how you're feeling. Then write three experiences from this past lunar cycle that have taught you something about yourself

and where you may want to evolve more. Proceed to write down three intentions you feel in your heart will help you fulfill your heart-space.

4. Read what you've written down out loud to Grandmother Moon and place your journal upon your altar space to amplify the intention. You can place selenite upon your journal to keep it protected.

5. Place the cup or bowl of water in the moonlight to charge the water for an hour or as long as you please. If you have any sound healing instruments you can play them above the water to amplify it as well. Remember, energy travels through water, so loving intention is key when handling the water. (The water will become amplified even if you cannot see the moon.)

6. Place your fruits and seasonal flowers upon your altar-space as an offering to the wisdom of the moon and as a sign of gratitude to Mother Earth. If you're calling in a different Goddess make sure to call upon her out loud so she can approach and receive your reverence with love to guide you forward within the ritual.

7. Take the plant medicine of your choice and place it into your hands as you close your eyes and listen to your intuition. What feeling arises when you hold this plant medicine? Breathe this feeling in deeply and expand it throughout your body one breath at a time, then breathe the feeling into the medicine. Invite white golden light into the space to provide protection for receiving this medicine into your body. (You can also use the moon-charged water to drink and connect deeper to this energetic frequency of the moon.) If you are using Hapé, make sure you are giving the medicine with deep loving prayer and intention and if you have never used Hapé before, have someone experienced speak to you about it beforehand so you know if it's right for you.

8. As you sit with the medicine, breathe deeply and make a humming sound on the exhales to invite a loving heart vibration into your body. You may want to close this ritual with dancing, singing, or with a cathartic self-soothing cry depending on how the moon is making you feel. Embrace all the energy, Goddess.

9. Lastly, take the rest of your moon water and you can either; pour it into a bath to soak in this powerful energy; place it into a squirt-bottle to amplify your home or cleanse your crystals; place it on your altar to

amplify your intentions; or drink the rest to nourish your blood.

10. Close your ritual by placing your seasonal flowers, pine cones, leaves and petals into a jar or a bowl to dry on your altar. You'll want to save these gems as you gather more throughout the season on each full moon. (I usually save these earth-gems throughout the year and on the final full moon cycle, I will read back all my intentions I set throughout the year and place all of the seasonal gems back into the lake as a sign of peace and natural order.

This is a beautiful way to close out your year and reflect upon all the lessons Gaia and the moon have gifted you with along the way.

There are many other possibilities and creations you can add to this ritual, but you can always use this as a guide to connect deeply and set a space that is supported for your healing and celebration of each lunar cycle, which gift us with different energy each time.

Side note: * Each lunar cycle is guided differently depending upon where the moon is located astrologically. You may want to research your natal chart as well as which zodiac sign the moon is currently travelling through to get more information on the energy its providing at this time. This will gift you with you more insight into what tools to use for this ritual as well as how the energy is currently affecting you. The more we learn about astrology, the more we are realizing it is an ancient philosophy that goes far beyond just a horoscope reading.*

NEW MOON RITUAL

I lay deep in the nest of my own reflection.

The darkness on this
night is shown
within me
as I go in and in
to reflect with her.

I feel the need to be lost once again.

I never assumed it would be easy
but this night is where I lay and feel
the waters that rise and fall
deeper and deeper.

Tonight I cannot live without the waters…
Nor can I hide.

Unaware of where I'm going
but listening and feeling to what needs to be embraced
and surrendered once again.

She speaks to me through emotional pain
neither bad nor good.
She shows me the layers
of purification I need to embrace.

I burn and surrender the past
that will no longer serve me as I move
along the path deep into her forest of faith.

I will not hold onto that which keeps me small.
It will not define me.

Grandmother hides… and I am happily lost.
Only to find myself within her glory once again.

SEASONAL NEW MOON RITUAL GUIDANCE

A great way to open a ceremony is an altar placing and blessing.

Ritual Ingredients:

> Crystal centrepiece altar of your choice [depending on the astrological space of the moon at this time].
> Incense / sage
> Goddess Nest Oracle Cards
> Paper
> Pen
> Lighter

To begin your new moon ritual, you'll need to understand the significance of the new moon. Once every cycle, the moon goes into hiding and this resembles our subconscious mind and our need as women to go inwards into the darkness to reflect, embrace and release that which is no longer needed. We usually come out of this time with revelations and much needed clarity. The moon teaches us that there is a time to shine and a time to rest.

So for this reflection period, what is it that you're feeling? What do you need to reflect upon in order to embrace more of the darkness in your subconscious? During the new moon, our ritual is focussed upon intentions to release the old and embrace the new. So let's begin by lighting your sage or incense and let the smoke dance and embrace your energetic space. A beautiful song to begin your ceremony with is: The Legends of Lemuria by Deya Dova.

Once you have set your space with the crystals of your choosing (usually in alignment with the astrological positioning of the moon at this time) take three deeps breaths with your eyes closed, then take out your Goddess Nest Oracle Cards and place them in your hands. As you feel the energy of the cards, ask the Goddess to show you what has been healed and what needs to be released. Run your fingers through the cards and chose a past, present and future card: Three separate cards. Place the first card on the floor in front of you to your left, the second in the middle and the third to the right.

The card to the left represents what you went through this past lunar cycle and what you have been working on with yourself to heal and grow. The middle card is the present card and it represents what you are currently learning from and working towards. Lastly, the card on the right is your future card, which will be your outcome if you fully dedicate your time to working with the present card.

You may want to write down any messages the oracle card reading has presented you with and read the full descriptions of the oracle cards here in 'Elevation 4' on page 128.

After you have read the messages the Goddess has gifted you with, begin to write down your intentions for releasing the past in a journal or on a piece of paper.

Take as much time as you need to genuinely feel into these intentions to release your past. This is a powerful practice to consciously release yourself from any low-vibrational energy that is holding you back from radical transformation.

An additional option to close this ritual is to burn your written intentions in a bowl or a fireplace (a safe space) where you can let the smoke dance and recalibrate emotional chaos back into love. This is a sign of a 'reset' in your life: The future is now clear to create what you wish and the fruitful lessons you have learned from your past will guide you with love.

You can close this ritual with a beautiful song called Stabat Mater by Libera - Hope. Finally, with with how it feels to release the past and send it love and forgiveness. This is how we can embrace all that we are, without denying it.

See your past for what it is, it does not define you and can be released or embraced at anytime.

Blessings, sweet Goddess, I hope this ritual serves you.

ELEVATION 4: ORACLE CARD WISDOM & INTUITION

Have you ever chosen an oracle card and the message resonated so deeply that it changed your perception of life? This is the magic of communicating with the Universe. The Universe loves to speak to us in ways that allow us to be open and receive.

I believe the most important part to meditation or intuitive guidance is to let go of our own preconceived notion for a specific answer or outcome and to simply allow the Universe to speak fully and completely without boundaries.

When we are fully willing to surrender our own visions of what is right for us, we can fully open to receive what is the greatest good for everyone involved. When we choose acceptance and surrender and give our intentions over to a higher energy, we are able to receive the natural course of creation. Just as nature does not strive or push to achieve its own magnificence and natural order—we also do not make everything happen on our own. We can let go of our ego's need to control outcomes and simply listen to the natural order of the Universe.

In The Goddess Nest Oracle Card Deck, this ceremonial form of guidance is also a way to increase our trust and connection to the Goddess within. This is a practice of simply letting go and allowing the messages to flow from the Law of Attraction.

The best way to use this oracle deck is to first hold the deck in your hands and make contact with each card by running your thumb across the corners once the deck is stacked. You can hold the deck in your most prominent hand and tap it three times with the other hand to give your energy and intention to the cards.

Once the deck has been consecrated, hold the cards within your palms and close your eyes. Take a long breath in and out as you focus your awareness just below your naval. Notice the feeling that is currently living here and expand it into your energetic heart centre. Breathe three times and then listen to the intention that arises from within.

Try to keep your intention or question open to possibility without contriving or making it too specific. Ask the Goddess to speak through the cards in ways that you can fully understand and resonate with. You can also ask the Goddess to allow you to be a channel of her light and honour her message with her support and guidance along the way.

I often receive the most potent messages from this oracle deck when I am fully in a place of not knowing what to do or how to feel. When I don't know how to process my emotions, I find it best to give up my intellect and fully allow the oracle cards to speak through my heart.

It is in the moments of complete desperation where we can find truth. When we are willing to ask for help and stay humble… we are given powerful wisdom. This usually is most impactful because we more are open to a form of guidance that is beyond the boundaries of our greatest imagination. When we are willing to give up the mind, we give the Goddess space to speak.

These oracle cards are filled with the poetry provided in this ritual book, which are meant to embody a prayer to help you integrate The Goddesses' guidance and also feel the essence of her wisdom.

You can embody these messages by writing the prayer down or by keeping it close to you when you feel the need to remember your hearts guidance.

To choose a card, begin to shuffle the cards lightly while you hold your intention within your heart. If a card chooses to fall from the deck, know that this card has a strong message for you. If you feel the call to keep shuffling and choose more cards, choose the ones that you feel most attracted to energetically and that are easily available to pull from the deck.

If a card is too difficult to pull, it is most likely not meant for you at this time. Once you feel the cards you've pulled are intuitively enough, lay them in front of you and read them from left to right as they will create a story and work together to provide a personal message.

To pull past, present and future cards, simply shuffle until your intuition tells you it is done. Pull the top three cards and lay them in order from left to right. The card on the left is the card from your past and what you had to undergo to get to where you are today, the middle card is what you need to focus on presently to get to your higher-self, and the card to the right will show you where you can potentially be if you work on yourself in the present.

The following pages provide an in-depth look into what each card may mean for you. Although the guidance is provided in more detail here, the best part about oracle card reading is that you are communicating directly with Source and the Goddess through your own intuition. Trust the first message that comes up for you as this is how we build trust within ourselves and grow our sense of intuition.

It is my prayer for you that these cards provide a sense of comfort in times of need, a sense of celebration in times of joy as well as a sense of freedom in times of rest.

I want to thank my sisterhood for being featured in the artwork on these beautiful cards. It is an honour to design them with the intuitive sense that the Goddess was celebrating all the work we've done together over the years.

To purchase the Oracle Card Deck, please see the last page of The Goddess Nest book. Enjoy reading these insights and may they bring you the ultimate guidance to awakening the Goddess within.

The following are descriptions for each wisdom oracle card you choose.

All my love,
- Ananda Cait

SELF LOVE

{PRAYER POEM}

"I break away from the fear of being abandoned
and I enter Heaven here…
within myself…
in this touch.

It's like falling in love for the first time
and quenching the aching need
for my own attention."

{DESCRIPTION}

You may have pulled this card because you're feeling disconnection from your own self-care and love. It's time to go within and listen to what you need from your own awareness. Self-care and creating a deep lasting relationship with yourself takes time and deep reflection. Ask what you are needing from yourself today. It may be time to rest or to simply feed yourself with nourishing foods. It may time to learn how to make love to the Goddess within by spending time touching and embracing your body. Show yourself acceptance by being sincere and sensual with yourself. If this feels silly to you, you definitely have some work to do in this area. Creating a sensual and deep love for yourself is what creates a world around you that reflects deep love. When you love yourself deeply and know how you like to be touched, admired, loved and known — the rest of the world will reflect this back to you.

We have grown up in a society that tells us self-love and care is shameful: Let's not neglect our need for our own touch and love. This is the time to really dive-in and awaken the Goddess who craves your deep attention and tantric awakening. Bring this prayer with you to remind yourself of the deep love you have within and set a tantric fire that will raise your vibrations so this energy can be reflected back to you in forms beyond your greatest imagination.

LIBERATION

{PRAYER POEM}

"Soft candied skies reflect in my halo
of liberation and belonging.

Shining an effervescent glow
from the Goddess' roots onto
this newly placed crown."

{DESCRIPTION}

It's time to do what makes you feel excited and free again. What makes you feel like you're being adventurous and connecting with your tribe? This is a sign to dive back into what truly makes you happy and what makes you come alive into your higher-self. This could be travel, taking a course to learn something new like painting or poetry, going to a yoga retreat to connect with like-minded people, spending more time being playful with friends, going to an ecstatic dance or trying something new at home.

Whatever it is, try to learn something new and step out of your comfort zone so you can break away from the mundane moments for awhile. Life is asking you to actively place yourself into situations that will allow your spirit to shine so that you can become more liberated, passionate and connected to the higher realms of existence.

Awakening the Goddess within sometimes requires us to be courageous and to step into unknown worlds that open our eyes to new frequencies. It's time to ignite this fire within once again so you can claim your higher-self and attract others into your life that are also working on themselves.

Have fun and enjoy life! It's time to let go, be playful and celebrate all the opportunities available to you. What a blessing!

I AM LOVE

{PRAYER POEM}

"I am the colour of deep gorgeous fuchsia pink that wraps around everything and everyone I love.

I am the Goddess that reminds you how good it feels to be alive."

{DESCRIPTION}

Goddess Venus is calling! She is letting you know that you're ready to share the love you have with the world. You are ready to step into the world to truly express this love without being shy and this is a true blessing to receive the bliss-point of the Divine love within.

You are ready to expand into a higher love, one that consists of a healthy give and take of friendship, sisterhood, business relationships, romantic partners as well as with animals. It's time to shine the love that you are so that you can turn every part of your world into divine loving gold!

Remember, we tend to go to a place that can separate us from love because we are human, but it is not about staying in the energy of love all the time, it's about how quickly we can come back to the energy of love and exercising this muscle daily.

In order to attract and expand more love in your life, you must be willing to give away the love that you already have. The best way to do this is to keep your auric-field vibration high and heart chakra balanced. Take care of yourself with nourishing plant medicines like cacao and other gems that lift the spirit. When we can be the love for others, we can receive ten-fold that which we put out into the world.

BE the LOVE that you are, sweet Goddess and celebrate the love that surrounds you. You are a powerful vessel of light.

SURRENDER

{PRAYER POEM}

"The waves rise and crash in my chest
as I continue to hold space…
simply to allow.

The grace of the Goddess holds me here.
She is a reflection of my
pure inner light of awareness."

{DESCRIPTION}

What has been bothering you, dear Goddess? It's time to work on your willingness to surrender into the Universal light. Give what energetic wave is weighing on your heart to the Universe and ask that it interpret it for you so you can learn from it and evolve consciously. Hold space for yourself to feel these lessons within because your heavy feelings are trying to tell you something.

Meditation, singing and sound healing will help assist you into these deep waters. There is a strong message waiting for you in this heaviness. Ask your angels to have you embrace these feelings and release them so that you can live in a lighter energy.

You can surrender your fears and triggers. Once you understand them better and gain more clarity you can act from a place of consciousness to resolve them. How can you integrate their lessons and come from a place of love when creating a solution? Remember Goddess, our triggers are our greatest teachers. They show us where we need to heal and call in the Universe in order to become a lighter being.

This is the work the Universe would have us do. Go into nature and let The Mother hold you with all your intrinsic emotion. She is the one who can truly help you if you surrender to her and ask her for her unwavering support. Then as the Goddess to show you where you need to surrender and evolve. This is a powerful practice — one with the opportunity to truly up-level into your higher-self. Surrender to the Goddess, she is trying to tell you something.

CLARITY

{PRAYER POEM}

*"Each and every experience inside
my heart is profound, unique
and purposeful."*

{DESCRIPTION}

Wow Goddess… this card brings very potent energy. You have connected deeply to the wisdom of your heart and should be very proud of the work you have done to get to where you are today.

You have taken the time to awaken into the moment of magic that ignites you by being a student of the Universe and listening to all her signs. You've dropped into your heart energy and have now begun to be fully led by a higher-calling.

You are a Goddess of service and light and you have made some difficult decisions in the past to let go of people, places and things that will no longer serve you and your journey forward. You are led by a conscious energy to thrive and be in the mind-set of abundance! Because of this consistent work you engage in, you are beginning to see the fruits of your conscious labour. You are currently birthing a new life that is more connected to the Mother and you are letting go fully of societal norms and expectations.

You are connected to the presence of beauty within you and the lessons that grow from your connection to intuition is a blessing. You are someone who has gone through hardship many times and have come out the other side to see the good in every moment.

We call this a 'full-circle-healing-moment' and you can feel an expansion arising like something is on the horizon awaiting you. A chapter has ended and a new one has begun. When you look back five years from now where were you? Write a letter from your higher-self about how proud you are of you and how far you've come. This is the product of your deep devotion to the Goddess— know that she has been with you all along is celebrating your journey!

BLISS

{PRAYER POEM}

*"Resting in the garden of faith
she lays her head on a blanket of stars…
she sips from a honey jar of sweet nectar
nourishing her veins of purity."*

{DESCRIPTION}

Goddess, have you experienced bliss lately? You may be currently experiencing this bliss and what it truly means to connect to the Goddess and Source. In this place you may feel happy for absolutely no reason. You may have recently taken up a consistent meditation practice, morning routine, ritualistic practice or have taken time to slow down and taste the fruits of life. You may be currently taking time to connect to a specific Goddess and she is now leading you into her wisdom so you can embody her essence. The Universe is holding you in this sweet space of luxurious laughter, sweetness and lightness. Enjoy these gifts, Goddess —— After all, you are the Universe in ecstatic motion!

Alternatively, the Goddess may be asking you to take more time to enjoy your life. Let go of your constant struggle or fight to succeed and celebrate the wins you've already claimed. You also may be asked to simply let go of your work and seriousness and find a way to enjoy the moment without grasping for a goal. Sometimes enjoying life means not gaining anything from it: There is no goal but this. Bliss is the simple pleasure of smiling and feeling gratitude to simply be alive.

Remember that you are the Universe coming to life to experience itself in all forms and emotions. Stop playing small and allow yourself to fully experience your authentic-self and tap into the sweetness of the moment. ——just as it is. It is your birthright to experience the 'Bliss-Point', but you must be open to it and make time to expand and elevate into it. This is the journey inwards and it is beautiful and glorious—truly something to look forward to.

MEDITATE

{PRAYER POEM}

"I rest gently in the steady flow
of this glowing cocoon.

I listen beyond me and hear
the sweetgrass singing into a chorus
of hymns I once heard long ago…"

{DESCRIPTION}

Meditation is the key to understanding and becoming more aware of the Goddess within. This is a sign to take some time to create a meditation practice that serves you and heals you. How do you like to connect in meditation? A great way to begin is with a guided meditation so that you can train your mind to slow down. We all have access to the ability to slow down and go within to receive messages from the Universe. Once we can learn to quiet the mind, we can begin to listen to the heart and what it needs in order to flourish. The heart and Source are not loud because they do not come from a place of fear. They come from an energy of all-knowing and so they do not have a need to yell at you, but in order to hear them we must quiet the ego and the mind.

The golden wisdom and joy we search for in our external lives is within our ability to consciously breathe, slow down and sit in stillness and silence. This practice takes time to become enjoyable at times and will be different each time, but if you dive into silence, it will show you things about yourself you were not aware of. This is the quickest way to advance the state of your mind, heart and spirit connection.

A great way to begin is with an altar space, sound healing and with some self-love rituals. Then allow yourself to sit in stillness anywhere from 5 - 20 minutes. Set a timer on your phone or clock and let the Universe take the time away from you. You can then drop into the nothingness and truly begin to connect. Envision yourself in a place that makes you feel safe, happy and completely free. Call in the Virgin Mary, Goddess Isis or Persephone to hold you here and share the secrets of the Universe with you. Be open to what you see, feel and hear.

AWAKENING

{PRAYER POEM}

"Resounding messages offered
deep in the heart of my most
vibrant dreams.

Taking me through timelines of
bright projection like a
movie-scene disconnected from
the storyline of my life."

{DESCRIPTION}

Goddess, you are beginning to awaken into your higher-self. You are owning your past, present and future and becoming the woman the natural course would have you be. You are letting go what you think you 'should' be and you are becoming your natural, beautiful-self. Awakening is not easy and requires the courage to go deep into our shadows and the darkness of the Universe. We see things we don't always want to see about ourselves, but in the awakening we will remember that all is exactly as it is meant to be and when we trust in the journey, we are able to become a strong channel of light for ourselves and for others. .

You are now understanding that you are perfect, whole and complete just as you are. There is nothing you need from any other human on Earth. No one can hold you like the Universe and the Divine Mother can. We can have gratitude and love others deeply, but in the awakening we let go of our inner-child's need to be seen and we surrender into the consistent divine love from the Universe that is always with us. Trusting this process completely, we free ourselves from the struggle of becoming something or reaching for external sources of happiness.

Whether you have just begun on this path or have been travelling through conscious space for a while now, you are learning more and more about who you truly are. Your authentic and unique gifts are becoming more apparent and you are able to share this with the world in small and large ways— keep moving along your journey and stay curious with every step.

SELF-WORTH

{PRAYER POEM}

*"Her avowed royalty
blood washes her clean
and grants her darkest
moments of seduction."*

{DESCRIPTION}

It's time to call in Goddess Kali. She is reaching out to you to revamp your self-perception and treat yourself with more respect. You are the Queen of your world and she wants you to know that you have the power to release anyone or any situation that is not contributing to your greatest good.

Goddess Kali wishes to be called upon when there is a darkness that needs to be cut out from your life and recalibrated. She is a compassionate Goddess that wishes only the best for you and if called upon, will place a circle of protection around you, only allowing the highest good to be attracted and lifted into your auric-field.

Once Goddess Kali is called upon into your life, expect yourself to set healthy boundaries and make difficult decisions in order to respect and love yourself more.

Goddess Kali represents the essence of the rose. She is the Queen of her garden and is powerful enough to change her entire existence without apology or mercy for what does not serve her anymore. You must be ready and willing to call her in, in order to face some harsh truths and realities that will allow you to be uplifted into a higher-realm of consciousness.

You will begin to feel more self-worth and honour for your existence and therefore, will be unwilling to tolerate energy that is not reflecting back to your divine value. It's time to level-up and step into the light of the divine Goddess Warrior of Compassion and Truth.

RITUAL

{PRAYER POEM}

"I am the Universe
coming to life to simply experience itself
transcend all the glory that exists here
in the dream of the mind."

{DESCRIPTION}

The Universe has a gift for you, Goddess. It's called the art of ritual and it is one of the most potent prayers the Universe could give us. Our ability to consciously connect to the Goddess and Source is so special that we have the opportunity to create something that calls-in what our soul desires: the full expression of the heart.

When we engage in ritual or ceremony, we are actively communicating with the Universe to say, " I am ready to receive your gifts of enlightenment and truth. I am ready and willing to enter the bliss-point of feeling the divine in true beauty with reverence for this life."

This action also allows us to be grateful for the connection to ourselves, to each other and to be in the energy of unconditional love. When we can take time to engage in the art of ritual, our entire world changes little by little. We begin to see messages and visions of where the Universe would have us go, whom it would have us meet and what it would have us say to the world.

We become a channel and a messenger of light consciousness that beams brighter with each dance. Ritual is a way to dance in mindful meditation and create a space that is safe to spiritually elevate with essences we want to connect deeper with. You may choose to focus on a teacher, a dieté, a form of expression, the Goddess and many others Gods and archetypes. This is a way to fully enliven parts of yourself that live within the Universe and create a sense of enlightenment.

A great way to get started with ritual is to follow the steps within The Goddess Nest book and heighten frequency within your living space, your mind, heart and soul connection — one ritual at a time.

PRIESTESS

{PRAYER POEM}

*"Finally the moon would
share its secrets with me.*

*Honouring my awareness
of its magic."*

{DESCRIPTION}

The Priestess is the Goddess that is ready to share her wisdom and step into her channel of service to the Cosmos, fully and completely. If you pulled this card, you are ready to step into your Dharma.

A Priestess helps other women honour their beauty and guides them through ceremony and conscious elevation to allow Shakti to rise within. A Priestess is not only inspired by the divine feminine, she embodies it fully and is ready to guide others to walk the path as well.

If you have pulled this card and do not feel ready to fully step into this role, take it as a sign that one day you will be ready. It's time to do the work and accept the hand of the Universe in its want for you to help others rise into the Goddess essence they have within.

Keep taking steps to nourish your garden within so you can learn, embrace and embody your conscious elevation into the Goddess so you will be ready to guide others.

This is your path and your purpose and it can be done in an infinite amount of ways. There is not one path forward to inspiring and guiding others… it could be by simply being your best-self and allowing others to be inspired by that, it could be to hold space for others in ceremony or to host retreats, write books and so much more.

Once you have fully embraced and embodied your divine feminine, you will be ready to share what you know and feel. This is a sign that you are very much ready to take this journey forward.

SENSUAL

{PRAYER POEM}

"With the pulsing of my womb
in a cosmic climax,
my heart breaks open with a wave
of emotion seeping from my eyes."

{DESCRIPTION}

Woo! It's time to set the tantric fire within and make love your essence, Goddess! Your soul is craving a deep sensual connection of love — in turn, you will also call this in from a Beloved partner. When you learn to make love to yourself, you begin to understand what sets your world on fire and how your body loves to be treated. The more you know how to treat yourself and your world with a tantric sense of deep desire, the more you will know how you wish to be treated by a partner and also how to dive deep into the delicious senses of the Universe.

You will begin to notice how the world makes love to itself each moment and how the sacred act of sensuality is the very point of creation and should be honoured within ourselves and within the world around us.

If you need a starting point to get more comfortable with the idea of making love with yourself, you can dive into some tantric teachings as well as kundalini teachings. The first step to fully accepting your journey to sensual blessings is the surrender of shame, sorrow, guilt and shyness. We must be willing to fully step into the tantric fires of bliss if we wish to experience the all-consuming energetic wave of the cosmos. You were created from sex, sensuality and the gift of pleasure. It's time to claim this essence and feel into your own dreamy kundalini awakening.

This practice will also help you to accept and honour the sensuality of others without shaming them. Our society would have women condemn each other, instead of lift them up for being sensual and proud of their bodies and souls. If you get triggered by other women's sensual desires and actions, it may be time to dive-into this wound within and heal any sorrow or shame that has been built and confirmed by the culture we live in. It's time to let all shame go… and dive deep into pleasure.

FAITH

{PRAYER POEM}

"I trust fully in the
process of life to care for me.
I will not be angry with myself.

For this is not needed
along the path to transformation."

{DESCRIPTION}

Your faith with the Universe and the Goddess is what will bring you the most peace within your life. Take time to think about your faith… what do you believe in? Are you open to a higher power and if so, are you truly willing to be guided by it and surrender your ideas of life to it?

It's when the Universe holds out its hand to you and you are ready to trust it 150% when it will say, 'ok, she's ready.' It will send you experiences, teachers, clients and lessons that will reflect what is beyond your wildest dreams. The Universal energy does not reflect what your ideas are… it is an energy of infinite possibility and a direct reflection of your heart-state.

Usually when we are not in an energy of faith and trust, we fall into a low vibration of fear and anxiety. This card is a sign that it is time to call in a higher power — maybe an archetype you have not worked with yet — in order to strengthen your faith in creation. Remember, we do not need to be religious or spiritual to have faith in an energy… we can simply remain open to the possibilities and trust in our intuition.

Let faith guide the way and don't worry about your need to control every aspect of your life. The acorn does not 'try' to turn into a tree… it is taken care of in the Universal natural order. When we let the natural course of things take place and we simply pray for the highest good for everyone involved — and we act when we receive signs and messages — the best outcome can then be available to us. Faith provides wins and abundance for everyone. There is more than enough to go around, there is more than enough love for everyone, there is an infinite amount of goodness in the world, but the key to experiencing it all is, yup you guessed it, Faith.

PRAYER

{PRAYER POEM}

"Help me to hold this pain,
to sit with it,
ask it questions,
be aware of what it means,
and understand where it
lives within my body.

I know I can heal and
meet my higher-self
with the help of my angels."

{DESCRIPTION}

Meditation is listening to the Universe and prayer is speaking to the Universe. Ultimately, this balance seems to work best within our communication to the Cosmos.

But the key to prayer is staying in the light of gratitude. By releasing our stipulation of an outcome for a prayer, we can remain open to what the Universe has in store for us.

One of the most powerful prayers to wake up to from *A Course in Miracles* is:

"Where would you have me be, what would you have me do, what would you have me say and to whom? What miracles would you have me perform today?"

This prayer is so powerful because it frames your mindset upon the act of service instead of expectation and it allows the Universe to be your guide for the day. This means that you will see all encounters with people as holy and all interactions with the world as either a call for love or an act of love. The key to prayer is to remain open to messages that you may not expect and to ask the Universe to steer you back into the essence of love when you need it most. Rely on this help to be your guide and remain an open channel without the need for the ego to control the outcomes of life.

INTUITION

{PRAYER POEM}

"I trust you great spirit within
let us dance together
along my path of glittering stars.

Lead me beyond what I currently know
and show me self-trust
the further I go."

{DESCRIPTION}

Our intuition is our greatest tool to connect with the Universe's messages for us. Understanding that a path or answer to a situation is personalized just for you, not for everyone. This is why we cannot rely on other people to tell us what is inherently right for us. The Universe knows what is the best possible route for you and it will communicate this through your gut instinct. It takes time for us to learn how to truly trust in our own decisions because as children we grew up constantly looking to other people to tell us right from wrong. Now, as an adult, you have the power to say yes or no.

The key to learning how to trust yourself is ultimately to increase your faith in the Universe and feel its wisdom within your body. When you are asked a question to do something or to make a decision, it is important to take a pause and step back to feel what your body is telling you. Not intellectually — but with a primal feeling.

Feelings are different from intellectualizing and analyzing a situation. When we connect to our intuition, we release the need to analyze the details of a situation and we can tap-into how we feel within that moment. The feeling could be angry, sad, nervous, excited, joyful, passionate, free, light, heavy, distraught and well… you get the idea. Sometimes our feelings do not make much sense logically to the mind and this is why they can be difficult to fully trust. But with time, the more you trust little-by-little you will begin to understand what the feeling means. Trusting in your own intuition can completely change your life and your peace of mind. If you can trust yourself and your connection to the Universe — you will always have the tools you need to thrive in life.

TRANSFORMATION

{PRAYER POEM}

*"The rose set a tantric fire
within her that resounded for centuries
breaking down patterns of harm…*

Only to worship herself once again."

{DESCRIPTION}

Have you been feeling like you have been in a cocoon for the last while? Well… change is on the horizon, Goddess. It will soon be time to spread your new glorious wings and celebrate life once again. You've been listening to the cosmos and holding space for energy that needs to be surrendered.

Many people think that transformation only happens once within our lifetime, but this is absolutely not true. We transform as humans many, many times. We may not always be ready to transform once again, but the Universe knows when it is time for us to change and elevate.

Like the river of life, we can flow with this change easily if we are willing to trust that it's all in the trusted hands of the Cosmos for good reason. The mirroring-test when we are transforming is the best way to elevate. Being able to observe ourselves without judgement when we are triggered by a situation allows us to understand why certain situations bring up emotional pain for us. Again, this is a personalized journey, so our triggers will most likely not affect other people.

Transformation is all about having the courage to witness our ego-mind so we can heal and increase awareness of our existence. This process teaches us to set down our external need to blame or deflect and simply go inwards to learn about ourselves. Once we can embrace the darkness (which will come up again and again) we can tame our dragons (our triggers) and begin to use them as transformative tools to listen, observe and respond to life. You are ready to elevate once again, Goddess, and this journey is one more step towards your greatest version. Keep going and know that the transformation you seek is currently being embodied.

VULNERABILITY

{PRAYER POEM}

"Goddess,
I bow to all that you are.
I love you so much.
You. Are. Divine."

{DESCRIPTION}

You are ready to step outside you comfort zone and get a little silly, a little playful and you're ready to show yourself and the world the real you. All the parts of you that you once thought were not acceptable or worthy of being celebrated, actually are your greatest characteristics. The more vulnerable we are willing to get with ourselves and the world, the stronger our relationships can be and we can begin to shine our true light. People can connect to authenticity and this is why being vulnerable is so powerful.

Are there parts of you that you are still just not willing to express? Take time to feel into the parts of you that embarrass the ego-mind. Your ego may be saying, 'this is silly' or 'you're not pretty enough to do that.' Well it's time to set your ego down and say, 'listen, I know you're trying to protect me from the world, but I don't need protection from expressing who I truly am. I am proud of who I am and I am comfortable in my own skin. I don't need to rely on the approval of others. I love all of me in all of my own phases and I am worthy of showing my true-self to the world."

Sometimes our ego just needs 'a good talking to' in order to quiet down. The ego loves to drive the 'car of our life' so it can have complete control and keep us small. It's time to take the steering wheel back and express yourself in ways you haven't in a long time. Whether this is making funny faces at yourself in the mirror, dancing by yourself or with others, truly getting honest with yourself on how you'd like to change or elevate in life, sharing a secret with a friend or a story that you've been ashamed of all your life. Understand that when we shine a light on the parts of ourselves that we've deemed shameful in the past, we become free of the fear-based prison our ego has created. All emotional debts can be lifted and we can truly begin to create a stronger relationship with ourselves and, in-turn strengthen our connection with others.

SISTERHOOD

{PRAYER POEM}

"Heart to heart we cradle
each other in violet skies
that gently fade down
into the ground.

You're ok now, I say.

We're ok now."

{DESCRIPTION}

Sisterhood is our primal birthright as women to be embraced in. When women gather, the entrainment process of their cycles sync-up and they create a new heightened frequency of their own … together in unison.

The energy of the tides and the connection of our genetic systems allows us to tangibly be connected to the unseen energy within us all. We as women have gone through centuries of pain, abuse, and ancestral trauma. When we come together and share our stories, we can ultimately see ourselves in each other, feel acknowledged and heard and we can safely heal in the knowing that we have each other no matter what.

Conscious sisterhood comes from a place of divine love. If you've ever felt the connection of women speaking from a place of deep emotional inquiry and connection you will know that there is no love or embrace on Earth like the love of our sisters. We understand each other from a deep primal heart-space.

In archaic times, the women would gather and help raise each others babies, they would bless each other with soft embraces and hair-play, they would help each other organize and listen to the stories they had to share with each other from the heart. They would spend hours and sometimes days together, while the men went out to hunt for food. As time has passed women have lost this much needed connection to each other because we do not live in tribes anymore. When women come together and truly listen from the heart, they recognize that they can be intimate with each other platonically by simply giving each other the affection they desire. The divine feminine is found in connected sisterhood where we can embrace our moon-side, our passionate and creative side, our sensual side and our need to be affectionate and heard.

This can truly change the way we view ourselves and the world around us. Women are so influenced by the modern patriarchy today and we are not honoured or revered as much as we were in ancient times. If the world were to understand that women go inwards during moon-cycles to gather fruits from the darkness and wisdom from Grandmother moon to bring back into the Earthly Realm to help humanity, we would be revered and honoured once again. But because this is not the case, women must recognize this within themselves and within each other.

There are many ways to connect with a conscious sisterhood. Red Tent ceremonies are becoming more and more popular once again throughout the world. This is a safe haven where Priestesses hold space for women to gather and speak deep from the womb and even express themselves with their blood. Some circles simply talk about their stories and read from the book: Women Who Run with The Wolves, as there are many metaphors for the collective connection women have within this book.

As women we have a very special gift to connect to the tides of the moon within us each month. We have the ability to become so sensitive that we can feel the collective sadness and healing within the Universe so that we may grow and elevate to become more compassionate beings. We also have the ability to become incredibly creative through art and sensual connection in all that we do. Without the divine feminine connection, there would be no flowers.

Sisterhood is so crucial in order to honour all the phases that makes a woman a powerful sorceress. Our magic can only be understood by others who have experienced it themselves. So connect with your sisters, dear Goddess, and revel in all the wisdom, emotion, affection and deep love they have to share with you. This is the magic of being a woman. Enjoy this journey and let the divine feminine essence embrace us all.

RISE ABOVE

{PRAYER POEM}

*"I am in awe of her
conviction to soften me,
pull me in,
again and again.
I sync up with her cradling rhythms
and roll into a new dawn."*

{DESCRIPTION}

It's time to rise above, dear Goddess. What does this mean to you? Have you been reacting to situations in life, instead of consciously responding from the heart? This is a difficult thing to master, but when we ask the Goddess within to guide us in our actions we can come from a place of power, instead of lack.

Sometimes it's very easy to complain and focus on negativity, especially when we are surrounded by other people that do this as a way to simply connect. We must train our minds to become more focussed on the blessings of our life and rise above the hardships of life that would have us believe there is not much good in this world.

Whenever you have a fear-based thought, simply say to yourself, 'I forgive this fear and I choose love instead.' This mantra will allow you to refocus your mind and strengthen your love muscles.

Observe the thoughts you mainly have throughout the day. You may want to take a full day to observe and write down all the tiny fears that come up for you. Once we can write our fears down on paper, observe them and read them, we can begin the process of separating our true selves from our ego-mind. We can begin to see the silly stories our ego makes for us in order to keep us small and unequipped in life. Once you have written and read these fears back to yourself, you can forgive each fear and begin to feed your love muscles in your mind and starve your fear-based thoughts.
Learn to nourish and feed your loving thoughts consistently and one day you will be able to come from a place of love without the need to consciously work at it.

ACCEPTANCE

{PRAYER POEM}

"A white cloak of light
lands around my limp body
showering me with
the blessing of truth."

{DESCRIPTION}

If you pulled this card, you may have recently felt the power of acceptance and letting go of the reins. When we can accept ourselves, people and situations fully just as they are right now, we give away the heavy energy we are holding onto and the need for things to be different than they are.

Acceptance and surrender are the answers we receive routinely in meditation and in the messages of the Universe. Our need to change things comes from our fears and painful illusions. We are all on a journey in life and our souls have asked to learn lessons exactly in the way that we currently are. We must honour other people's journeys whether we agree with them or not. We also must accept our own journey because this is how we have asked to learn in this lifetime. When we accept that everything is in divine order, we can let go of our preconceived notions of life and act from a place of divine order and support.

This all comes back to the idea of not having to feel all the sadness and hardships of the world in order to empathize with it. We do not need to take on all the darkness of the world in order to be of service or support. We can be the lighthouse for others by living in the light and not taking on the low vibrational energy that surrounds us.

SHADOW WORK

{PRAYER POEM}

"I learn to seep deep
into the wisdom of this great awakening
once again.

Learning to stop the judgement
of my own demise.
For I have died a-thousand times
and always come back to life."

{DESCRIPTION}

It is time to go into the darkness, Goddess and return with gems of clarity, purity and healing. When we can sit with our demons, we can grow in an untimely existence that lets us evolve into our authentic-self.

What part of your soul and emotional-self are you denying to look at and give attention? Your shadow work will be the key to releasing old habits, old ways of thinking and feeling as well as allowing you to feel lighter and more creative.

Shadow work is some of the most difficult work we will ever undergo within our lifetime. This is why many people shy away from it and refuse to sit in stillness or truly feel their pain. This type of work requires learning how to hold space for yourself without judgement or fear.

When we can sit in the fire of our energetic waves of emotion, we can be sure that we are transforming and levelling up in life. See this as a blessing and move forward as a warrior of the Goddess. It's time to take a deep breath and ask yourself the hard questions within that you have been constantly distracting yourself from.

Remember that there are many levels of growth within this life. Just when you think you have healed and moved on, the Universe will show you another part of yourself that needs healing, but if you can be conscious enough with the pain to support your healing, you will walk through the fire not only unscathed, but with a new set of wings.

NEST

{PRAYER POEM}

*"I am so grateful for us
as I hold space here
simply to allow."*

{DESCRIPTION}

Your very own Goddess Nest is waiting! Whether it's with your sisters or on your own, it's time to set up a space where you can feel safe to heal and celebrate your essence. To begin, think about what type of luxurious items you would like to surround yourself with. It could be as simple as a photo that reminds you of a moment that made you happy. If you'd like to get a little more creative with your Goddess Nest, you can lay out a cozy blanket on the floor, couch, bed or ground outside and place throw pillows. Roses are the highest frequency flower, but all flowers bring a sense of high vibrational energy.

Another high-frequency item to use are crystals. There are many different intentions used with different types of crystals for example: Rose quartz is the Divine Mother energy for self love and blessings. Quartz holds the crown chakra intentions and jade provides a calming frequency. You can use amethyst to help with grieving and connecting to Source. You will want to feel within your heart which crystals you are attracted to within the moment and ask them for assistance in your healing process along your journey.

Essential oils bring a sense of reverence for the body and can be a powerful way to ease into the moment. Lavender is a luxurious oil that is great for calming the nervous system, Ylang Ylang is a beautiful oil that creates a sense of romance for the moment. Sandalwood is used for grounding and rose oil is used to bless the Goddess essence. Again, the choice is yours!

Take pride and great intention in building a nest that is in alignment with how you're feeling and cradle yourself in this space where you can adorn your body with the blessings of self love. Read a book, take a nap, give yourself an oil massage, yoni steam or paint, write and listen to music. So many options!

WRITE

{PRAYER POEM}

*"The poetry poured through my blood
and casted a spell on this
illusion of destiny
showing me a painting of no boundaries
no paths…
no signs…*

*Just the Astral Plane
where there are dreams I've never seen."*

{DESCRIPTION}

This practice is so cathartic to the mind, heart and body. When we write feelings or thoughts down, we are releasing them physically out of the mind, body and heart and placing them out into the physical realm to be released or manifested. Writing with intention is a powerful ritual that moves energy through the body and into our journey forward.

This can be a therapeutic practice, but it can also be a powerful way to connect to the Goddess and Source. Try meditating for 5 - 10 minutes and at the end (still in silence) take 10 minutes to free-write. Free writing means placing pen to paper and writing without thinking.

This means writing down anything that simply comes through right away for you. Write without stopping, even if it doesn't make sense. You may be surprised at what comes out onto the paper. Thoughts, emotions and feelings that were being denied, or you may just get a letter from the Universe.

The Universe is asking to connect with you through the art of words and feelings. This is a powerful practice to connect, release and reflect. Read the words back and underline what resonates with you. This may be a message for you presently or for the future. The Universe has a very tricky way with divine timing, so keep your eyes open to the signs it provides.

GRATITUDE

{PRAYER POEM}

"I woke up with the answer
of the stars who took my hand
and guided me out
to the other side."

{DESCRIPTION}

Have you ever engaged in a nourishing gratitude practice, sister? The Goddess is asking you to set your sights on all the blessings that are always in your life. Even if it is the smallest parts of life, like your head on a cozy pillow and the feeling of soft sheets covering your body.

When we focus on the good, the good can grow. Take some time to let go of your worries and each morning write down 2-8 things you're grateful for in this life presently. The Goddess views this process as nourishing the inner-garden of life.

Raise your vibration and focus on saying thank you to the Universe for the small things in life. This allows us to feed our love muscles a good, hearty meal of LOVE.

You can even post your gratitude list on your fridge or somewhere you'll see it often so you are always reminded of the many blessings and opportunities you have in this life.

We are blessed in this life, sister. Sometimes we just forget.

LISTEN

{PRAYER POEM}

*"I hear the call of the rare,
unique jewels in the ancient
feminine spirit."*

{DESCRIPTION}

Wow, Goddess! This card is a sign that it is time to stop whatever you're doing and take time to listen to the Universe. It has potent messages that are ready for you to receive. This is a time in your life when the messages you receive will resonate and your conscious mind can apply the wisdom to your existence.

When you receive this card it is a sign to slow down and listen. There is abundant treasure within the silence that could potentially change the course of your life. You may be at a fork in the road and feeling either a little stuck or you are moving so fast you've forgotten to take time to feel into your intuition.

When we can take time to listen to Source, we can begin to align ourselves with the stars. Set up a space where you can just slow down and begin to listen to the silence from which everything is birthed from.

There truly is gold in silence. Are you ready to receive?

SERVICE

{PRAYER POEM}

"The Earth's acclaimed sisterhood
arrives to her side
with deep purpose."

{DESCRIPTION}

To be in the energy of service is the most abundant place we can grow from. This card is a sign that you may be analyzing or focussing too much on what you need to receive from the world around you. It may also be a symbol of opportunity to ask how you can contribute to the people and community around you.

We tend to run stories over and over again in our minds about the past or the future. Whenever we are in a state of panic or anxiety it is coming from a place of fear about the future or the past and this can take away your precise gift of presence.

First, write down all the blessings you have and all the wonderful attributes of the people in your life. Then, close your eyes and feel the blessings fill up your cup. Then, decide to get out of your own way and plan ways to be of service to your world.

You may be able to go clean up a park nearby or do someones laundry for them. You may be able to cook someone dinner or pay for someone's groceries. You may call a friend or a loved one to tell them you love them and want the best for them. All of these small acts of service fill our cup back up to feel abundant and to get out of the storyline that life is not going our way.

Feel into the moment of what is calling you today to be of service for someone. Start with small acts of kindness and once you feel more abundant dig deeper into the moment and make a plan to create more love in your world by giving without expectation—-This is the key to feeling at peace within yourself.

DREAM WORK

{PRAYER POEM}

*"Resounding messages
are offered deep in the heart
of my most vibrant dreams."*

{DESCRIPTION}

Our dreams sometimes can give us clues and insight into our greatest passion and desire in life. They can also give us clues about what the body is trying to release and heal.

Try not to analyze your dreams too much because sometimes the body is just ready to release some energy and when we sleep this is a great time for the body to release. If we analyze too much on a dream that did not feel good, then we can end up placing that energy back into the body and undoing the healing work. On the other hand, you may have a dream that is so vibrant and resonates so deep with you that you wake up feeling so inspired and peaceful at the same time—This dream may have a powerful message for you.

Sometimes we dream about animals or colours or places that bring us great peace and joy. You may want to look up the symbolism for what you saw in the dream or keep a dream book beside you so you can write down how the dream made you feel. Animals have come to me many times in my dreams and they usually are very vibrant colours. The symbolism of animals in dreams can unlock messages that you would not have embodied without learning from the dream.

Writing the dream down in a journal will help you remember it wisdom and when you receive a symbol in life that is similar to the dream —- you'll have a diary to look back on and confirm that the Universe is speaking to you through your dreams. The Yellow Butterfly Poem is about a dream I had once about a powerful, large yellow butterfly that guided me home to where I currently live now. Keep an open mind and an open heart so you can truly experience the magic of your dreams.

PATIENCE

{PRAYER POEM}

"Treading softly.
I go slow.

I rest gently in the steady flow
of this glowing cocoon."

{DESCRIPTION}

Your dreams have been realized and you want to make them happen. Ah yes, Goddess this is an exciting place to be. There are many open doors for you to walk through and you can choose any door you'd like.

However, whichever door you wish to walk through has a long journey behind it and you must be willing to stand the test of time to create what you desire to give to the world. There will be many lessons and teachers and experiences that will align you with what you're currently manifesting and being a humble student will be your greatest asset when walking the path forward.

Patience and virtue are two important attributes to embrace. Although the ego does not align with this thought process, it can be a great learning skill to sit in the essence of patience. Breathe into the feeling of patience. What does it feel like for you? To not have everything realized so quickly? Do you feel a deep fire burning within you to move swiftly and eagerly along your journey? —-Good.

Keep that fire burning along your path forward. This is what will allow you to keep going, but just know, whether it's in the interest of your career, your relationships, your friendships or in your daily life of moving through tasks, along the path forward, the Universe will test you time and time again to make sure this is what you truly are ready for. If you show emotional maturity, patience and reverence for divine timing, the Universe will co-create with you. If you decide to take the reins away from the Universe and move forward on your own… you will only be able to go so far.

Patience is a virtue. TRULY!

FORGIVENESS

{PRAYER POEM}

"I look into the bright new
colours facing me now
healing and cleansing me of my past
—- showing me forgiveness."

{DESCRIPTION}

Have you ever given away your need to be right and just decided to forgive and let go? Have you had to work on forgiveness in the past?

The best way to forgive… is ultimately to give yourself permission to be human. To let yourself know that you are doing the best you can everyday with what you know right now and so is everyone else.

We are all humans going along the same path in life… Meditate on the act of forgiveness and compassion. If you are wanting to forgive yourself for your past, envision a beautiful waterfall of light washing over your scalp and down your temples to the back of your neck. Allow this light to take over your energetic body and envision it healing and cleansing all the way though to your heart-centre to your tailbone and down to the centre of Mother Earth.

Allow your energetic parents to hold you here in their unconditional love and healing powers. The Universe loves you and knows that you are an innocent child of God and creation—no matter what you've done in your past, you will always be an innocent child of creation. You can heal and move forward by forgiving your past and by simply letting go of any shame, guilt and resentment for your actions or thoughts… you can reclaim the light right now and choose to move forward with kindness, compassion and grace for yourself. Sit in this light and allow it to take over you for the grace of God. Invite the Goddess in to awaken and enliven your being.

Once you have felt this self-compassion moving throughout your body, you will then have more loving energy to place into the world around you. The path is yours, Goddess. Take it with kindness and give yourself the forgiveness you deserve.

INDESTRUCTIBLE

{PRAYER POEM}

"Something in me
came alive from the numbness
to fight for me."

{DESCRIPTION}

You have been on a difficult path in the past and you may be going through something right now that is very challenging. It's not easy to walk through the fire that burns with us when we need to elevate and grow.

Like the caterpillar growing something new in its cocoon… the discomfort and the pain that comes with transformation will soon bring you into your light. It's hard to see the light when things are so dark and gloomy, but the Goddess wants you to remember that you are strong and have come this far.

Do not give up because you have so much beauty within you that it's trying to come up to the surface. In order to truly become your higher-self, you must understand what it's like to crumble, fail, falter and struggle. Your story will be your message.

If you're feeling helpless or hopeless, remember to speak to the Goddess and your guardian angels. They are always waiting to listen to you and assist you along your healing journey. When you can co-create and co-heal with the Universe by your side, you will be indestructible. Invite a higher energy in to assist you with what it is you're currently feeling and remember, the darker the night, the brighter the morning.

The more pain we go through, the stronger we become. Your angels are here with you and the Goddess wants you to know, she is listening and ready to come to your aid whenever you're ready to call upon her. It's time to ask for assistance and know that the co-creation process you undergo with a higher power will ignite many other forms of strength within you.
Sending you blessings and healings, Goddess. There is always an energy waiting within you to fight for your highest good. Trust in this and give yourself the hope and faith that you deserve.

PURE JOY

{PRAYER POEM}

*"Gliding and singing
to a chorus so beautiful…*

Like I've never heard music before."

{DESCRIPTION}

Wow Goddess! You radiate pure joy and it's easy to vibe with you. You have been filling your cup and treating yourself right with all the love and connection your heart desires and the rest of the world can now witness this love glowing and beaming from your heart and auric field.

Have you ever looked into someones eyes and you can see a light behind their gaze that is electric? That is you right now, Goddess. Shining with radiant, pure joy that only can come from within.

If you chose this card right now, it could mean that you are currently making shifts in your life that align with how you want to feel and live everyday.

You're making conscious choices to be at ease and flow with the river of life without the fear to hold you back any longer. You may also feel like you're currently in a space that supports your spiritual journey and are meeting new friends that can reflect this back to you in a positive way.

Pure joy is not always the goal and it certainly does not mean we need to be joyful all the time… but it is nice when we can honour a joyful-state it is necessary to be aware when we are happy so that we can remember the what this feels like.

A great way to cultivate more love and joy in your life is to keep a jar full of written blessings. When you think of a moment you were joyful or grateful, write it down on a piece of paper and place it in the jar. Everyday go to this 'Joy Jar' and pick out a written joy card. Read out loud to yourself and close your eyes to take in the vibration. Take a breath and come back to that energy whenever you feel the need to.

LIVE IN THE HEART

{PRAYER POEM}

"It was the Yellow Butterfly
that showed me this place.

To be in the essence of sensual living."

{DESCRIPTION}

You have made it to another chapter of your soul life, Goddess. Do you feel the blessings and abundance that have graced you thus far? You have been hard at work for a long time. You have been diving deep into your darkness to claim the light that is rightfully yours and the Universe is well aware of the work you've been doing.

You are currently allowing your heart to lead the way and you take time to fully quiet the mind and dive into how you feel about situations, instead of using your logic for everything. Our ego would have us believe that the heart is unrealistic and emotional — however the heart is the direct portal to feeling what the Universe has in store for you. You know this, Goddess and you've been surrendering to this energy and acting when given feelings of excitement, passion, love and joy.

You have come a long way from a broken heart to an awakened third eye and here you are living in the truth of your heart. This is a time to truly just revel in your own personal created heaven. You are living your greatest desires and although there is always more work to be done and truth to uncover about yourself, you are already feeling grateful and blessed to be living the life you have worked so hard for.

Enjoy every second of it… there was a time you prayed for all you have now.

I AM ENOUGH

{PRAYER POEM}

"And I repeat this hymn
into my golden years.

I am…
I am…
I simply am."

{DESCRIPTION}

The most powerful mantra we can give ourselves is the mantra: 'I am.' Anything that comes after 'I am' is what your reality will be.

We all live by intention, whether we are doing this consciously or unconsciously. Whatever you believe about yourself—is ultimately your reality. This means you have the power to change whatever your current story is about yourself. This opportunity to unveil the true you (a pure inner light of awareness) is so spectacular and powerful because if you can just get out of your own way and understand that you are more than enough to claim all your deepest desires… your dreams will begin to come into form.

So, why are you enough? Well… we all are. We all were born onto this Earth in the very same energy that created us. We also all have the power to cultivate cosmic energy whenever we please. Why? Because we are all a part of the cosmic creation. We are all a part of the Universe—and the Universe is infinite, abundant, generous, unconditional and ever-changing.

You are a part of the Universe. Your bones are made from the very same frequency as the stardust that glows on us night after night. The stars may seem lightyears away… but they are also right here within us. You are enough and you deserve more than you've desired in the past. You may have given up hope to experience certain things in your life, but The Universe wants you to know that you are worthy of whatever your heart desires… you just have to awaken by telling yourself, 'I am. I am. I am here. I am worthy. I am enough.' Read the poem called: 'I am Enough' and it will help you along this journey inwards to claim your self-worth.

FULL CIRCLE HEALING

{PRAYER POEM}

"The sun-showers open around me
and I lay in this sensual healing."

{DESCRIPTION}

It's time, Goddess. Have you recently felt a remembrance and a coming home energy within your heart? You have practiced your shadow-work in the past with force and now it is time to let go of the heavy work… Celebrate all the love you've embodied!

You have let go of your inner-child's need to constantly be 'seen' or 'recognized' by other people in order to feel of value. You have healed and forgiven many of the traumatic events you've faced in the past and you have had some deep moments of crying and holding space for yourself in order to elevate, open your mind and your heart space.

You may have gone through an entire decade of healing and shadow work and are now finally feeling like you've healed some major past traumas and are ready to step into a comfortable and authentic expression. You are ready to celebrate, relax, feel good and let go of the healing process for now.

But don't worry, love. There will come another time down the road of your life to do more shadow work and healing, for now, you're able to call-in and manifest anything you wish for and truly appreciate it.

Be proud of yourself for truly doing the work and elevating to a place where you can genuinely love the person you are today! You deserve all of the glory! Congratulations. This is an energetic graduation to a new chapter of your life that brings you back to who you truly are and always have been: A Goddess of love.

FEEL

{PRAYER POEM}

*"I want to sit with you forever,
my dear heart."*

{DESCRIPTION}

Let's dive into the solar plexus; The space in-between our ribs where we all process our emotions. What is coming up for you, Goddess? There is an emotion here within your body that is needing to be felt and seen.

Take some time to feel and hold yourself in a loving space so you can process some emotions that have been held in for far too long. If we hold onto our emotions and do not let them out, they tend to manifest into a low vibration. All emotions come out in different ways, if we do not process them in a healthy, proactive and conscious way, they may come out through irritability, annoyance, destructive anger, self-sabotage, anxiety, panic attacks and many other outlets the body likes to use.

If you are needing to process anger, truly give yourself permission to feel it and process it though a fire-element action. This could look like screaming into a pillow or doing some running, dancing ferociously, kick-boxing or screaming in the forest while you run into the ocean like a wild animal. However you want to feel your anger in a healthy way, try not to feel shameful about it. Anger is a normal, human condition that especially women are told not to express—this is societal abuse that is placed upon us as women and we have every right to fully feel, express and process our emotions in a healthy and conscious way. This will ultimately make you feel much lighter and happier the next day.

Anger and sadness both stem from fear. So once you've felt these emotions fully through your chosen proactive activity, take time to reflect upon what you are fearful of. Feel the freedom to cry and show yourself compassion. This is the blessing of being able to feel all of life's expressions and healing our own trauma.

WELLNESS

{PRAYER POEM}

*"This devotion and gratitude
feed my body like potent water
accumulating into Prana."*

{DESCRIPTION}

Let's heighten your vibration, Goddess! Nourish your body and heart with the pranic life-force from food, drink, plant medicine, resting, inspiration and loving care.

When you treat yourself well with nourishing supplements, you are amplifying your energetic field, which attracts more of what your heart desires. Why? Because you are treating yourself as if you already have everything you desire. Remember, 'like-energy' attracts 'like-energy.' So if you are feeling down and in a low vibration… you will be attracting experiences, people and events into your life that are also low vibration.

The good news is we all have the power to be the energy we wish to be surrounded with. The first way to amplify your auric-field of subconscious energy is to meditate, stop any intake of alcohol or stimulants (of course, keep taking the medication you need to survive), and allow yourself time to exercise, do yoga and take pleasure in creating things just for the fun of it.

You may enjoy doing Reiki, or painting, writing, singing, dancing or gardening. Whatever your creative outlet is, try to make sure it does not have the goal of receiving anything monetary. We can water our energetic garden of vibration by simply BEING, instead of DOING. Try not to intellectualize your creations all the time and simply be in the presence of your own beauty and in the act of creating. This is what nourishes your soul and amplifies your sense of well-being. This is when the Goddess essence can rise up and influence your decisions towards living your purpose.

Beautiful is a woman in alignment with her creation and sense of well-being. Treat yourself right and you will manifest more of what you already are and more of how you feel. Up the vibration, sister!

INNER-CHILD

{PRAYER POEM}

*"Rest my sweet child…
for my patchwork of aligned stars
lives within you."*

{DESCRIPTION}

"Hello, little girl… the little child inside that has been asking to be nourished and disciplined. You've been looking for a parent who is loving and supportive but also gives you boundaries so you know you are safe."

If you've pulled this card it's time to work specifically with your inner-child for she is calling out to you even though she is scared, shy and untrusting. Right now, she needs you to take time to go inside and find her where she is hiding. Take time to meditate with her, dance with her, create and be silly with her. Show her that you are here for her to be playful, supportive, loving and also let her know that YOU are her parent. No one else can give her the love she needs like you can. Let her know that what served her in the past to remain protected and safe will no longer serve her now. Once she feels safe enough to open up and express herself out in the world, you will be able to dance together along the path of life and create, love and be more vulnerable with the world. You've got your own back and no matter what happens, your inner-child will know she is safe to be herself.

If you are unsure about where to start for inner-child healing work, ask the Goddess to guide you inwards to find her and feel your inner-child through meditation and consistent acknowledgement throughout the day. Remember that your inner-child has wisdom too, so give her the attention she deserves when she shows up in life… but also have patience with her when she comes from a place of fear. Fear is her experience and sometimes she comes from a place of expectation so you can gently tell her it's safe to rest and to not be fearful or be needy. It's time to step up as the parent for yourself and show your inner-child that she has a Goddess looking out for her—-No need to worry anymore, little one.

NEW BEGINNING

{PRAYER POEM}

"Feeling my body come alive
one rainbow drop at a time
softly kissing my skin."

{DESCRIPTION}

New beginnings are so exciting, Goddess. Maybe you're feeling a change of location to live or travel coming up soon. You may be feeling a change in career or hobbies. You may be coming back into your sense of feeling and artistic expression or maybe you are embarking on growing a family and homestead.

All of these areas of your life could be shifting at the same time! There are so many possibilities when it comes to a new chapter and we can get swept up in the excitement of it all without setting conscious intentions for the present and future.

Take time to do some rituals and write down what you're feeling. This is needed to grow and elevate and come into alignment with your higher-self so that this new chapter can be streamlined towards your greatest good for everyone involved!

A great practice is to first write down three blessings you're grateful for from your present and past. What did you have to overcome in the last chapter to get to where you are now? Then write down presently what you're focused on. What do you feel you need to work on in order to elevate consciously and energetically? Would you like to learn a new healing modality or take a course on meditation? Get clear on what you would like to focus on because the more clear we can get upon what we truly desire, the more the Universe can resonate with this as well. Try to feel into these intentions from the heart, instead of your head. A beautiful prayer for this type of work is, 'What is meant for me will always be for me. And so I relax into the knowing of what already exists.'

THE GODDESS CARD

{PRAYER POEM}

*"Her. She feels familiar.
I embody her truth and worship the rose:
The Queen of the Garden.
She is a reflection of my essence."*

{DESCRIPTION}

You're on the right path, dear Goddess because you picked up this book and are reading this passage. If you chose this card, the Goddess has had her eye on you for a long time and has desired to be called in by you.

She is waiting to guide you back into the heart to claim your sensual-self and your most authentic form of expression. Feel into this card and write down what emotions come up when you envision the Goddess within?

What does she currently feel like when you show up to a party or a gathering? How does she present herself through you when you're in a creative space of ritual or art or physical expression? How does she show up through your desire for certain clothing and adornment of makeup of jewelry or natural crystal selection? Are you guided more to plants and natural Gaia gems of adornment and nourishment of your vessel?

Are you more guided to Earth, Water, Air, Fire or Ether? All of these types of questions will lead you to honour the Goddess essence within that is personalized to you. You can begin to learn about the divine feminine archetypes such as the Wild Woman and The Archetype Maiden. Each essence lives within us and there are many of them. The more you learn about the Goddess and call her in, the more you can experience her along your own journey and create a personal relationship with all of her expressions.

This is an exciting journey to be on. Stay curious about how she expresses herself through you each day and call her in with ritual, ceremony, learning about her stories through books and ancient resources as well as taking some time to feel her within your body by touching, breathing, creating and moving.

BUTTERFLY

{PRAYER POEM}

"I place my emotions onto the
throne of creation and the bridge-point
that cradles my heart
with Heaven."

{DESCRIPTION}

In order to fly, we must be able to trust. In order to trust, we must be willing to let go of control and in order to let go, we must be willing to see things differently.

If you've pulled this card, you are ready to see your life through the lens of love. This means letting go of your fears that are keeping you small and allowing yourself to become lighter so you can fly and soar into a new dawn.

What fears have you been holding onto that you know are not serving you and are exhausting your higher-self? If you feel tired or weary, know this may be a sign that you are exhausting your energetic body by over-analyzing things and your ego is creating stories about your life that are an illusion. It's time to discipline the ego, and feed the heart.

If you feel like you cannot control a situation, but it is giving you anxiety because it's triggering you, simply say this out loud to your altar or throughout the day: 'I choose to let go of that which I cannot control and I give it away to God and the Goddess within to recalibrate and take care of.'

This way, you can let go of what you cannot control and trust in the higher power to enter into your life so you can become lighter and more free of any burdens. The butterfly knows that there is no burden worth carrying. The butterfly would die if they held onto something too heavy. In order to fly, we must be able to trust. In order to trust, we must be willing to let go of control and in order to let go, we must be willing to see things differently. Let Source show you the way — so you can fly high like the butterfly you were always meant to be.

THE ROSE

{PRAYER POEM}

"And the golden light
of the rose set a tantric fire
within her that resounded for
centuries, breaking down patterns of harm."

{DESCRIPTION}

The essence of the rose is calling you, Goddess. Since ancient times, the rose has symbolized Source at work in whatever situation they appear. The intimate labyrinth of the rose shows us our creator's active presence within the act of all creation. As the rose blooms, it gradually opens to reveal layers upon layers of petals ; representing the process of how spiritual wisdom unfolds in people's lives.

The scent of the rose is both sweet and bitter, reminding us of the power of love and its connection to God. Many miracles involving angels involve the symbol of the rose and the rose itself as an essence can speak to us as a representation of the Goddess within.

If you see a rose, take this symbol as a sign that a miracle is approaching and that you will be given the strength to transform into the pure essence of love, trust and wisdom.

Angels use rose scents as physical signs of their spiritual presence with people because roses have powerful energy fields that vibrate at a high electrical frequency—the highest of any flower on Earth.

Rose essential oil vibrates at a rate of 320 megahertz of electrical energy. Take the sign of the rose as a miracle and a symbol of a higher power trying to communicate, teach or celebrate with you.

RED TENT

{PRAYER POEM}

"The crown now rests
gently up my head.
I no longer sit at the foot of her
Palace, bur recognize her
entire Queendom
within my velvet flowing river."

{DESCRIPTION}

The Red Tent is an ancient tradition where women gather in hidden sacred tents (sometimes for days) to release into the wisdom of their menstrual-cycle. Some women who were not on the cycles would simply join into the tents to gather in talks about Grandmother Moon and to talk about the wisdom they've received in the past through their cycles and current emotional states. These gatherings were celebrated as a time to connect in sisterhood and reveal the truth about their hearts. It was a sacred time that allowed women the chance to sync their cycles up to one another and to revel in the delicious energy of the divine feminine.

Recently, these sacred tribal tents have come back slowly into modern society and women all over the world are taking advantage of this sacred sisterhood. It's a time to be celebrated for being vulnerable and raw, and to release the past as we shed physical layers within the womb together like a flower that loses it petals, only to bloom yet again. If you've chosen this card, this may be a call to connect deeper to your menstrual cycle journey. You may want to connect with how you're feeling more often or engage in ritual upon the arrival of your moon. If you are in menopause, it may be time to connect with other women who have gone through menopause as well — there is still much wisdom to be learned from other women even upon 'completion' of our moon cycles. The moon is asking you to sit in the wisdom of your sisters to reflect and become more aware and connected with the wisdom the moon provides within this sacred time. The veil to the ethers is very thin for us when we go through our moon journey and it provides an opportunity to gain messages and learn more about ourselves as women.

ISIS

{PRAYER POEM}

*"She is the Queen
of New Eden
finally crossing the threshold.*

*Changing the ordinary world…
and revealing her heart."*

{DESCRIPTION}

Isis is a Goddess that represents fertility in many different ways. This card could mean you are on a journey to expanding your family, or it could mean the birthing of a new project, new home, new career or new friendships.

Whatever the case may be, there is a fire brewing within you to birth something (or someone) new into your life and this is happening very soon for you.

You may have felt an energy on the horizon calling your name as that feeling of something new is about to take place. Have you been seeing the numbers 555, 9:11, 1010 or 111? These numbers represent the closing of one chapter and the elevation into a new spiritual journey forward. Energetically, you are ready to take a new path forward in life to truly understand who you are authentically.

This may be scary, and may mean that you will need to make some difficult decisions when moving forward because spiritual elevation always means there is a sacrifice and a rebirth period. Trust in yourself and the Universe and know that if there is a passion and excitement around change, then it is time to move forward.

If you are feeling confused about the path forward, you can ask for a sign from the Universe. However, the ultimate task it going inwards to listen and feel within your body what you truly want. The more you can sit in meditation and write down the feelings that are coming up within you, the closer the bond you will create with yourself when making difficult decisions. Just know, there is a new life waiting close by for you to choose and prepare for its blessings. Ask the Goddess within to help guide you forward towards this new chapter.

MANIFEST

{PRAYER POEM}

*"And then The Goddess
showed me how to
fly to the moon."*

{DESCRIPTION}

It's time to manifest your dreams, dear Goddess. if you've pulled this card, the Universe is asking you to sit with your visions in meditation. The frequency we hold, is the frequency we attract!

Hold the vision of yourself doing all the beautiful work and meeting all the amazing people in your life through your meditations and sit with the feeling of living your best life. You may be surprised with the visions that present themselves.

It's important to hold visions in your mind and sit with them so we can see these dreams as natural and not outside of ourselves. Miracles are our birthright and they are never too far from us to reach, but we must believe they are a part of us, first. The higher you can get your energetic frequency by sitting with your higher-self visions, the more of a magnet you will become for your dreams to manifest into this realm of consciousness.

The other key to manifestation is to stay open to creative possibilities. Look back on your life and think of all the situations, people, and places you've attracted into your life. They were always manifested, maybe not in the way you thought they would be, but they arrived at some point in your life because you had a thought about it. These visions arrived in divine-timing and in the way that is best for everyone involved. This is why you do not need to over analyze or control your manifestations, just be open to creative possibilities and when in meditation stay open to seeing yourself living a life you've never dreamt of. Again, manifestation requires faith that the Universe is more ingenious than we are. It knows what is the ultimate highest-good for us… and so we stay patient while we sit in meditation to receive its visions so we can elevate in frequency and attract what we already are. Enjoy the playful process of manifesting, Goddess!

CHAPTER 5: LOVE NOTE TO THE GODDESS

It is with great pleasure and worship of the Goddess within to send this book out into the world to those who are aware and working consciously every moment to elevate their awakening journey. The conscious women I continue to work with have taught me so much and they are the star-map to my own healing journey.

I see myself in each and every one of them and I believe this is why the feminine archetypes have always resonated so deeply with me. These essences live within us all at different points within our lives here on Earth.

In my past, I was not only hurt by men, but also by women. And at some point along the way I demonized the woman ideology as someone who was in competition with me and was not consciously devoted to the sanctity of her tribe. I'm sure we all have experienced this at one point or another in our lives and it is through the healing work of the Goddess that allows us all to release our ego-mind and truly come into the raw and vulnerable place that creates a strong sense of primal-belonging.

Working with women has been my greatest journey to healing my own childhood wounds and I have engaged in these gatherings as a cosmic channel for the highest learning and teaching opportunities available for everyone who chooses to work with the light. I remain humble as I continue to learn from other women and honour them as they unveil their layers of truth and step courageously into their authentic-selves.

I have also had the great pleasure of meeting some of my mentors along the path to conscious freedom, and I've noticed that all their teachings have had one message in common: Only love is real.

This message has come into my life time and time again either through the teachings of mentors, or through my own meditation-work of releasing and surrendering. When someone decides to accept the divine feminine awakening process into their life, I know they have already awakened into a conscious being.

It is this work that allows them to stay open to the ascension process with a sense of curiosity, instead of expectation. When we call in the divine feminine within us to rise, we can use this energy to create a life that is a direct reflection of our hearts; one that keeps changing and evolving like a cosmic paintbrush gently and steadily flowing from one colour to the next to create something new.

When a woman asks the Goddess essence to rise within them, it is like saying to the Universe, 'I am ready to receive all of you so I can birth your mission through me and help the collective to awaken into softness and into their own acclaim'.

The power of this work has transformed so many to meet and embody their higher-selves and it has truly been the greatest treasure I have ever known to be true in my life.

As humans, I feel we tend to live with the goal of strictly receiving. It is for this reason that conscious work is so powerful because it requires us to be of service fully to ourselves and to the world around us. A woman who chooses to walk in the light of her truth and embraces her divine assignment to the Universe is an elevated woman… and this is why she is called a Goddess. She has done the work on herself enough to elevate into feeling the connection of divine love and therefore walks in the light of God.

This work takes time and much experience, but the truth of this work is to truly be able to remain open like a channel, while allowing the embodiment of surrender and acceptance.

I truly believe that the world's inhabitants are awakening faster now than ever before and this is why conscious spiritual work is becoming more and more available to us as a collective. It's truly wonderful to witness this gathered ascension as more and more women come together to greet each other with reverence and humility.

We have so much to learn from Shakti. She is an untapped energy that has been neglected for far too long, yet it is our birthright to embody her and use her transformative potion for all the world to be galvanized by—She is here and she is ready to rise.

It is my prayer that this book be used as a tool by Shakti to call out clearly to those who are ready to awaken through her grace. I believe that once we awaken, it is our duty to hold out our hand to others who may wish to walk the path of Source as well; this is why this book was written.

I also pray that those who embrace the divine feminine step up as leaders to support the ascension of the divine masculine in the world. I believe that the divine feminine is a powerful teacher in the Universe and with this potency comes much responsibility to hold our brothers in our arms with compassion and without condition. We must allow the men of the world to express their most vulnerable feminine emotions with love and celebration. Only then will both of these awakening divine energies be able to heal the world and be transcended individually within the human ascension process.

With each step forward along this spiritual evolution and with each person that reads this book, I remain relaxed and patient as the Universe unfolds before me and shows me the true beauty of witnessing what already exists.

It is with a deep bow that I honour your call to consciously awaken the Goddess within. Thank you for being here with me.

In perfect love,
In perfect truth,
We are all one.

- Ananda Cait

FEMININE & MASCULINE DIVINITY

"When a man chooses a woman who follows her calling, his only chance to maintain the connection is in following her... and above all in creating space for her to follow her own path. It may happen that he needs to abandon his own neediness, or that he finds a means of healing through their common path — but not in the gentlest manner.

When a man chooses a woman who heals the collective wounds of the women by following her calling, his 'Yes' for her equals a 'Yes' to a bigger purpose far beyond building a house or raising children. Their connection goes beyond fulfilling the classical gender role models. For this man accepts the job of having the back of this woman, of catching her when she cannot transform the pain of the world anymore. It means for him to welcome a different form of sexuality, since healing on the level of sexuality is one of the most profound issues of the woman who needs to become a healer. For him this, again, is about welcoming slowness, softness and healing — about holding back or redirecting his own drive... about being present for the whole.

Because when a man chooses a woman who aims for freedom, they can only achieve this together... and by him leaving his narcissistic aspects behind and recognizing the path of the woman as his own path towards freedom.

When a man chooses a woman who is bigger, he cannot dwell in the places of energies of oppression or of playing small. He — if he chooses to take on this mission with her — accepts a task serving the well-being of all men, even though it happens in the background. Within this background he creates space of security, of keeping her safe from an ambush bred by his own old wounds, driving her into submission.

When a man chooses a woman out of his fascination with her radiance and wisdom, it must be obvious to him that he cannot be stuck within his own deficits in a way that makes him want to diminish her radiance... purely out of fear of having to share her with others. When a man chooses a woman who follows her calling, he cannot fear these words: respect, humility and surrender. He will rather walk the path of divinity — alongside his woman, the healer with gratitude and an overflowing heart.

For such a woman will choose — if she ever needs to choose — in favour of the well-being of all women ...and she will choose walking her path alone instead of leaving it for him. Nevertheless, she is aware of the power that lies in the presence of a man who is beating the drum... for her."
~ Moksha Devi Sunshine

ABOUT THE AUTHOR

Ananda Cait is a poet, author, energetic channeler and international ceremonial guide. For years, she has held space for women all over the world to dive deep into their shadows and honour the Goddess within. **The Goddess Nest** is a direct reflection of the healing work she continues to conduct at home for herself and others, creating sacred havens to ignite spiritual awakenings and to revel in the playful celebration of connection. This book was channeled from Isvara: the infinite Universal pool of knowledge. Enjoy these prayer poems, mantras and rituals that have been collected from over 20 years of writing and channeling. This book is an offering of love.

The Goddess Nest is a healing book of awakening transcended and alchemized by Poet & Ceremonial Guide, Ananda Cait. It is an offering to be used as a ritualistic tool in creating sacred space (a nest) for the practicing Goddess to witness herself fully with unconditional love.

A Goddess Nest is a sacred space that a *conscious woman* creates for herself to conduct deep spiritual healing for self-actualization and the conscious celebration of life. *The Goddess Nest* is read by woman all over the world who want to awaken and nourish their Goddess essence through the power of prayer poetry, mantra & ritual. When you activate the words in this book you communicate to the Universe that you are ready to embrace your higher-self: The Goddess within.

As you surround yourself with the abundance you desire (flowers, candles, crystals); adorn yourself with these powerful healing words of prayer and mantra and prepare to dive deep into your very own **Goddess awakening**. Call upon your higher-self through the intimate ritual of self-reflection and the deep honouring of your heart expression.

Powerful ritual recipes for the Goddess are also provided in this soul-nourishing book to practice and remember your roots as you come back home into the sweetness of the heart. Rituals of body acceptance, connection to Mother Earth, plant medicine rituals, sacred sisterhood circles, as well as how to create spell jars and set deep intentions of forgiveness will all support you along your independent healing journey as well as in your desire for *embraced sisterhood*.

Whether you are venturing into deep shadow work or are looking to hold space for yourself in a luxurious nest of unconditional love, this book is a powerful tool that will ignite spiritual awakening by embracing all the faces of ones true-self: **The Goddess within.**

CONNECT WITH THE AUTHOR

Follow Ananda Cait on Instagram:
@TheGoddessNestBook
@AnandaSoulRetreats
@TheSacredBliss

Find Ananda's Free Ritual, Guided Meditation and Reiki Treatments:
YouTube Channel: @Ananda Cait ASMR

Connect with the more Goddesses who have read The Goddess Nest:
on Facebook Pages:
@The Goddess Nest Book
@Ananda Soul Retreats

Connect with Ananda for more poetry, Goddess products and healing work:
www.TheGoddessNest.com

Manufactured by Amazon.ca
Bolton, ON